Critical Acclaim for "The Peaceable Kingdom"

"This amazing book captivated me from the beginning to the very last sentence. Patton Boyle, once again, has managed to spin a thought-provoking, charming, and enlightening tale. At times, I had to put the book down to process the new ideas percolating through my brain, at other times, I could not stop reading. Some of the scenes are so beautiful, so powerful, that I found myself in tears. Well done, Patton! This story is a true gift to our world!
It was my honor, as well as great pleasure, to help get this amazing story ready for publication."

GC Sinclaire
Imaginative Fantasy Author (Arianna: A Tale from the Eleven Kingdoms, Mystic Highlands Love Story)

"This is a whimsical and thoughtful look at our spirituality and its boundless nature, offering a lot to ponder in a delightful way."

The Rev. Marilyn Wilder

"This thoughtful book is a combination of entertainment and possibility that shows the reader an alternative way to look at our journey inward. Patton Boyle challenges us to reconsider what we have grown to accept as the way life is - in our daily lives, in church, in how we relate to our spiritual side and what we show of it to the people we meet. Perhaps the things of which we are so certain mask a deeper reality that asks us to accept what we cannot prove."

John Hotchner

The

Peaceable

Kingdom

The Peaceable Kingdom

Patton Boyle

Printed in the United States of America

Patton Boyle
Wenatchee, WA 98801
pattonboyle1@gmail.com

The Peaceable Kingdom/Patton Boyle--1st ed.
Interior Design- GC Sinclaire
Cover Design – GC Sinclaire

Print Edition ISBN 978-1-7334524-0-3
E-Book Edition ISBN 978-1-7334524-1-0

And they shall beat their swords into plowshares,
and their spears into pruning hooks;
nation shall not lift up sword against nation,
neither shall they learn war any more.

Isaiah 2:4b

Author's Introduction

This book is a work of fiction; this introduction is not. Some years ago, after writing *Screaming Hawk: The Mystic Warrior* and *Screaming Hawk: The Mystic Paths,* I engaged in a sweat lodge ceremony with Howard Bad Hand, a Native American Medicine Man in New Mexico. It was a powerful and deeply meaningful experience. In the midst of the ceremony, Thunder Eagle, one of Howard's helper spirits, appeared to me in the sweat lodge as a luminous white cloud. Speaking through the medicine man as interpreter, Thunder Eagle indicated that he liked my earlier writing and its teachings but then went on to comment in great detail not only about some of those teachings but also about Light Beings and their functions, which aligned with passages that were already in the manuscript of this book, *The Peaceable Kingdom.*

This book is dedicated to Thunder Eagle and all the Beings of Light who make my writing possible. I wish to thank Marilyn Wilder and John Hotchner who provided encouragement and helped me correct the manuscript. I also owe a special debt of gratitude to GC Sinclaire, an accomplished author in her own right, who spent countless hours designing the cover and the layout, as well as editing my manuscript and preparing it for publication.

One further note, as a result of writing and subsequently reading this book myself, I became far more aware of the presence of angels, Light Beings, in my life. It is my hope and prayer that this book will have the same effect on others who read it.

CHAPTER 1

"Why have you come to us?" they asked silently.

The dazzling white light, in all directions, was so intense that, at first, Jonathan could not distinguish any objects from the background of light. Gradually his own being changed frequency from the courser oscillations of the physical realm he had left behind to the finer, more rapid vibrations of the dimension he had just entered. He discovered that he was in the presence of a group of ten or more Light Beings, angels, who had come to greet him. They used no words to communicate but conveyed their thoughts directly to his mind. Jonathan answered them in the same fashion.

"Why have you come?" they asked again.

"I don't know. I was simply meditating and seem to have arrived here."

"Are you the one?" the leader asked.

"What do you mean?"

"Are you the one we have been expecting?"

"I don't know. I told you what happened. All I know is that I am here."

The Beings paused as though they were conferring among themselves. Then the leader spoke again. "Do you seek *The Way of Peace*?"

"I have been yearning for peace all my life, but I don't know how to achieve it."

The Beings moved to and fro as though excited. "Are you a seeker of the truth for others?" the leader asked.

"Well, yes. In my profession I counsel with people who have problems and I share with them the insights that I gain."

That too seemed to interest them.

"How did you find *The Portal of Light?*"

"I don't know. The last few times I meditated, I found myself led to a gate suspended in space. Tonight, I entered the gate. That's what happened."

"What do you know of peace?"

"I know that I long for it, but most in my world are not able to achieve it. We do not have peace within, and we seem unable to live in peace with each other. Can you teach me about peace?"

The motion of the Beings increased dramatically.

"Remain here. We will discuss the matter."

The Beings faded from view and then reemerged almost immediately. "We have discussed this and find your request acceptable. We are uncertain about you being the one who is to come but, in any case, we are willing to teach you about peace. We ask only that you apply our teachings. You must live the truth even if you do not understand the truth. Are you willing to do that?"

"Yes."

"Good. That is what we require. We have decided to assign Azar to you. You will meet him the next time you come.

"First, Azar will teach you about us. True peace can come only if you join with our realm in the endeavor. Peace comes from a dimension beyond your own. We can teach you *The Way of Peace* but to utilize our teachings you must enter into an experience of our realm while you are still in your own. Many of the religions of your world refer to this, but people have not understood. They do not comprehend that it is the joining of the realms that brings *The Kingdom on Earth*. You must learn our ways, but you must also experience our dimension. When you experience our dimension in the midst of your own world, you will have peace.

"Do you understand?"

"No. I don't understand how I can experience, in my own world, a realm as different as I have found yours to be."

"That is good. For if you had fully understood, you

would not be teachable. Those who are teachable are those who can be confused. It is through confusion that the truth is conveyed, and it is through clearing the confusion that the truth is revealed. To convey the truth is different from revealing the truth. First we will convey the truth. Then we will assist you in its revelation. Between those two experiences you will usually experience some confusion. Expect that. It will happen to you often. Confusion is part of the pathway to truth. You are confused now. It seems impossible to join your realm with ours. What we are going to teach you is impossible. That is why you will be confused. To bring about the impossible, one must go through confusion. There is no other way.

"Learning *The Way of Peace* will be painful at times. To encounter one's inner nature usually brings pain before it brings joy. But if you and your people follow *The Way*, your world will be changed, and you can be the instruments to usher in *The Reign of Peace on Earth*.

"You must go now. We will answer no further questions today. Return to us tomorrow evening. Your next session will be with Azar. He will teach you about us and about our nature. Come to our realm tomorrow evening."

The Beings faded into the vast background of white light.

Jonathan left through the Portal of Light and became aware of his physical surroundings as the dawn was breaking in his own world.

CHAPTER 2

Jonathan slept and rested much of the day. That night he returned to the *Realm of Light*. When he passed through *The Portal*, he was greeted immediately.

"I am Azar. I was sent to meet you. I understand you want to learn about us and about *The Way of Peace*."

Azar looked like the other Beings of Light Jonathan had met the night before. His somewhat slender body was made entirely of white light. He had arms, legs, a torso and a head but there were no distinguishing gender characteristics. Although he had definite form he appeared simultaneously to be solid but not solid. Variations in the intensity of the background light could be clearly distinguished when looking through his translucent body.

Although Jonathan had noticed little difference between each Being's appearance the previous night, he had sensed that each had their own personality. Azar's predominant trait was that of profound, but sensitive, complexity. He had the qualities of a great man of science combined with those of a highly creative artist. Johnathan liked Azar instantly and felt very comfortable in his presence.

"I am here to teach you," Azar continued. "It will be easier for you to understand our teachings after you understand us and our realm. That is where we will begin.

"I have never before encountered one such as yourself," continued Azar. "I was, of course, aware of the existence of your realm, but my assignments in the past did not include encountering humans. It must be quite interesting to exist in a realm where one's actions are being constantly restrained by physical limitations and by what you call 'time.' I understand that being human can be quite frustrating and yet also, at times, very enjoyable. Perhaps in exchange for my explanations regarding our realm, you, in turn, could tell me about what it is like to exist in yours.

"When I was given this assignment, I was told that you had come to learn about peace and that you have already been told about the need to establish a link between your realm and ours. That, of course, is impossible so you will become very confused before the link is accomplished. You are undoubtedly already aware that the impossible can be accomplished if approached in the right manner. Are you not?

"This issue of time fascinates me. What is it like to live in that dimension? Perhaps you can tell me all about it. I have never existed in a realm where time exists. Since all things unfold for us simultaneously, it is hard for me to understand what it would be like to experience things sequentially. In some ways it must make events more interesting, but I can't imagine what it would be like not to have an awareness of the entire pattern of events. Is it true that you do not know what the results of a pattern are until time passes? How does time pass? That doesn't make sense to me.

"I understand that in your realm total peace has never been experienced. Is it true that beings in your reality actually try to exterminate each other? Why do they do that? That makes no sense to me.

"Peace does not allow the extermination of anything. Nothing is ever exterminated anyway. Beings can change realms, but they don't cease to exist. Is it really true that humans get into struggles with each other and cause other humans to change realms against their will? What is the value of that?

"Our realm, of course, is quite different than yours. You must have noticed some of the differences already. Do you like it here? I find it quite enjoyable. Of course, I can't really compare it to your realm, now can I?"

"Wait!" Jonathan sputtered. "Azar, you have asked me a number of questions and made comments that would naturally call for some sort of response from me and yet you have given me no opportunity to reply or even a chance to ask any questions of my own. Why won't you listen to me?"

Azar seemed puzzled. He paused for a moment, only a moment. Then he spoke again. "I find that strange. You say I do not listen to you. How do you know that? In our realm things are quite different from your realm. As I said, I have never been in your realm, but it seems to me that..."

"You don't listen to me," interrupted Jonathan. "You keep right on talking. You ask me a question and then you keep talking without giving me time to answer. It's irritating."

"Now that *is* fascinating!" responded Azar. "I have been told that one of my character flaws is that I focus more on myself than I do on others. It is interesting that that has come into your awareness. You experience it as me not taking time to listen to you. I do not experience time, as I said, so I don't experience things sequentially. All of our interactions occur simultaneously. For me, there is no such thing as waiting. But for you there is. And because time is a part of your existence, you experience things sequentially even when you come to our realm. You experience my character flaw as my not waiting for you to answer. Truly amazing! Perhaps you can be of great assistance to me. You experience my flaw directly. I can only experience it indirectly, which makes it very hard for me to work on it. Because you experience time, you can tell me when I am overly focused on myself. Of course, there is no 'when' for me, only 'the eternal now.' Perhaps it really is true that some issues can be resolved more easily in your realm than in ours. I was told that by our teachers, but I couldn't imagine how that could be true. This is so interesting!

"Will you help me with it, Jonathan? Will you tell me when I am overly focused on myself?"

Azar paused. He seemed to be actually waiting for a response.

"Yes," said Jonathan. "In fact, you just waited for my answer."

"I did? Now that's fascinating.

"When I was given this assignment, I was told that I could learn some things from you that would help me with my own development. At first, I didn't understand how that could be possible. But now I think I am starting to understand what they meant."

"Azar, you say that you experience everything simultaneously and yet you just said 'at first' you did not understand but 'now' you are starting to understand. That is sequential."

Azar glowed even brighter than before. "Now that is truly amazing! You understand me as speaking to you in sequential terms even though time does not exist in our realm. This may prove to be the most exciting assignment I have ever had!"

"You just did it again," said Jonathan. "To say that, this may prove to be the most exciting assignment you 'have ever had' implies that there have been other assignments in the past."

"I love it!" Azar exclaimed, as he swayed back and forth in obvious ecstasy. "I convey my thoughts to you, and they are translated into sequential terms because you can only experience things sequentially. Fascinating!

"But how can I precisely explain my experience to you? The meaning that is received by you is not exactly what I send to you in my thoughts. I guess there is no way you can fully understand what it is like to exist in our realm unless you can exist without time. But that option is not currently available to you. Even though you are now in our realm, you are not experiencing it in quite the same way we do.

"Johnathan, I will do my best to help you understand. But there are some things you will not be able to fully comprehend until there is a true merger of our realms. As long as you can accept that, we can proceed."

"I can accept that," said Jonathan.

"Good.

"Well, Jonathan, here goes!

"I can experience confusion. I cannot experience time, but I can experience an idea or concept as being both clear and not clear to me at the same time. I suspect that in your realm you would experience that as not understanding the concept and then later coming to understand it. What you experience as growth or changes that occur over time, we experience as clarity. Your primary task is to grow. Our primary task is to achieve clarity. The two are similar but not the same. There is no way to fully explain this to you, but I hope my attempt is helpful."

"Well, Azar, let me just say that it is both clear and not clear to me at the same time."

Azar seemed to like Jonathan's response. He swayed back and forth for a moment and then continued, "In order to bring peace to your realm you need to enter into a relationship with us and link your realm to ours. My job is to bring you to a state somewhere between total understanding of us, which is not possible, and ignorance. Somewhere between the two, a relationship can occur. You will know you have achieved that state of relationship when you come to love us. Having an interest in us or even liking us is not enough. For the two realms to become linked, you must love us, and we must come to love you. It is love that links individuals and realms, not understanding.

"But without some understanding it is difficult for healthy love to develop. Healthy love is between equals. You must come to appreciate that you are the equals of us and we of you. In order to truly love the Great Spirit of the Universe the same state must be achieved; one must come to love the Great Spirit as an equal. That is not to say that the Spirit is the same as you or the same as us. But to love the Almighty Spirit as an equal is what true love for the Spirit is all about. Hard as that may be to understand, the relationship is based on equality, not on subservience. Few in your realm have ever fully achieved that understanding. But that is what the Christ, the Buddha, and some others in your world came to understand. They attempted to teach humans how to relate to the Spirit as an equal. But they were greatly misunderstood while they were alive. And after they died, those in your realm tried to make them into special deities rather than coming to understand what they had actually taught. Their message was that all beings are part of the Deity. To love the Deity is to love oneself and to love oneself is to love the Deity. But one must be aware that the Deity is both separate from us and the same as us. When that level of understanding is achieved, true, healthy love for the Deity can be realized.

"But why, you might ask, am I talking about the Spirit when I am on the subject of linking our two realms? Both your realm and mine are the Spirit's realm. The Spirit is encountered in both. When you relate to us, you must do it from the perspective that we are all one in the Spirit.

"It is the Spirit's intent that our two realms be linked. We know that. It has been revealed to us, but we experience a lack of clarity regarding the characteristics of that merger. Because you operate within time, you undoubtedly experience that linkage as not yet having occurred.

"Perhaps the merger has not occurred because humans have so little direct experience of our realm. So far very few humans have ever come to our realm. It is far more common for us to enter yours. From time to time some of us are sent to your realm to fulfill some purpose or other task assigned to us by the Spirit."

"What is it like for you to come to my realm, Azar?"

"I do not know from my own experience. I have never been given such an assignment. Just as it is unwise for beings from your realm to come to our realm without a specific purpose, we are not allowed to go to your realm without a reason for being there. But I am told by some who have been on assignments in your realm that they found it quite enjoyable and that existence within the limitations of time and physical reality is rather pleasant, if approached in the right way."

"What do you mean? 'If approached in the right way?'"

"Well, it has been reported that most humans spend a lot of energy struggling against limitations rather than accepting them as gifts from the Spirit. Your purpose is to grow, to develop deeper character and to experience alignment with the Spirit. Limitations are quite helpful in promoting growth, but most people seem to long for an existence without limitations. That seems strange to us. Our realm is largely free of limitations, but I assure you that there are some very real drawbacks to existing without them. It is much more difficult to progress with one's character development in this realm than it is in yours.

"By the way, how have I been doing lately regarding listening to you? Have I been giving you time to speak?"

"Yes, you have. You have been doing much better with

that."

"That pleases me," said Azar, pulsing intensely.

"Azar, you said that there have been a number of visitations from your realm to mine. What form do they take?"

"Many times, those in your realm are unaware of our presence or of the ways in which we are assisting you. But sometimes we do allow ourselves to be recognized, especially in situations where we have a message of some sort to deliver. At times we are referred to as 'angels' by those in your realm. Actually, that word merely means 'messenger.' But being a messenger for the Spirit is only one of several types of assignments that may be given to us."

"What other kinds of assignments are given to Beings of Light?"

"Occasionally we are told to protect one of you from a particular danger. Sometimes we assist creative people by providing them with inspiration at a time when it is particularly needed. But more frequently, we are sent to assist in solving particular problems. In those situations, our presence is less likely to be recognized by those in your realm. And, oh yes, there is another function that we are sometimes called upon to perform, but it seems to be rather rare; we are sometimes asked to be present at certain religious celebrations that are particularly pleasing to the Spirit. I'm not sure why those assignments are so rare. Maybe the Spirit doesn't like most of your religious celebrations. Or maybe it is because in most of your religious celebrations you do not request the presence of Beings of Light. I don't know. But whatever the reason, being assigned to a religious celebration in your realm is extremely rare. I know only a few Beings who have ever performed that function."

"What do Beings of Light do when they attend a religious celebration?"

"That depends. Sometimes they are there to impart wisdom or give encouragement to the participants. At other times, they are there to help channel power for a particular purpose, like healing, or to assist the person who is preaching or conducting the service. I don't know a lot about this subject. As I said, assignments to religious celebrations are rather rare. My guess is that assignments would be more frequent if there were more sincere requests for our aid. One Being told me that most of the religious practices he had attended in your realm seemed to be people merely rehearing their previously held beliefs rather than engaging in a sincere seeking of the truth. The truth is not found in what one already believes; the truth is found in what one has yet to discover. My guess is that unless your religions make more room for discovery and growth, our encounters with your realm will continue to occur more often in other areas than in your religious services."

Azar paused and looked intently at Jonathan. "I do not have the limitations that you have. I could continue to talk for what would be, for you, a very long time. But to function in a realm that is not one's own can be quite draining. I may have talked too long already. I sense that you are becoming tired. You must return to your realm and rest or you will run the risk of becoming ill. You should rest for a few days before you return to us. There will be other opportunities for us to talk. You must go now."

Azar faded into the background of light.

Jonathan passed through *The Portal* and returned to consciousness. He was totally exhausted and immediately fell into a deep sleep.

CHAPTER 3

Jonathan rested for several days. He attended to the necessary tasks of daily living but deliberately rested when he had free time. When his energy had fully returned he entered the silence again and passed through the Portal of Light.

Azar was there to greet him.

"I am pleased that you have returned," Azar said. "Have you been in good health?"

"Yes. I was tired for a few days after we last talked, but I am feeling rested now."

"We must pay more attention to your limitations. We talked too long last time. When you notice your energy starting to decline you must tell me. I will also try to be more sensitive to your energy level. As you know, I am inclined to focus too much on myself and not enough on others. I am sorry about keeping you so long."

"That's all right, Azar. I should have told you I was getting tired. I was very interested in what you were telling me last time. Please tell me more."

"I will, Jonathan, but first I want to thank you. Your comments about your experience of me not listening to you were quite helpful to me. I have noticed a little more clarity within myself since your comments. Please let me know if I fail to listen to you in this session."

"I will."

"Thank you, Jonathan.

"Now, you said you wanted me to tell you more. What I am about to tell you is hard to explain to one who operates in the dimension of time, so please bear with me.

"We, in our realm, have always existed. We were created by the Spirit before your realm, but your realm too has always existed."

"I'm already confused, Azar. How could we have always existed if we were created? Creation in itself implies a beginning."

"I said that it might be hard for you to understand. Those in your realm are so accustomed to thinking in terms of time that you apply it to actions that do not exist in time. Creation is one of those categories. Creation does not exist in time. Or to put it another way, the beginning always *was*.

"Creation is not what you think it is, Johnathan. It is not the calling into being of things that did not previously exist. Everything that *is*, always has been. You always have been, just as I always have been. All that *IS* is part of the Spirit and has always existed. Creation is not the beginning of something; it is the redefinition of that which already *IS*. When we were created, we, as part of the Spirit, were defined as being a part that was different from any other part of the Spirit. But once that distinction was made, it always existed.

"The same is true of you. You are part of the Spirit. When you were defined as being a different part of the Spirit than the Beings of Light, for example, you were created, but that does not mean that you did not exist before your creation. You always existed. Defining something gives it separateness but that which *IS*, *WAS*, before it was defined as separate from that which it *IS NOT*.

"I can tell that I am confusing you. Let me put it another way.

"If you, in your realm, took a block of stone and carved it into a beautiful statue, you would be creating a statue, but you would not be creating what the statue consists of. You would be defining the statue into existence by removing the parts of the stone that were not the statue. The statue existed within the stone prior to your removal of the stone that surrounded it. You would have created the statue by defining what was the statue and what was not the statue and by separating that which was not the statue from that which was the statue. But the statue existed within the stone before you created it. Is that helpful?"

"Yes."

"Good.

"I have used an example from your realm where physical reality exists, and physical pieces of stone are chipped away in order to reveal statues. In our realm, which of course is not physical, a statue can exist in its creative form also, but we would not have to go through the process of chipping stone to produce it. But in another sense we all create in the same way. We Beings of Light create by redefining what *IS*, just as you create by redefining what *IS*, and just as the Spirit creates by redefining what *IS*. But whatever is created in that fashion always *WAS*. That is the nature of true reality.

"Is that clear now, Jonathan?"

"Yes, it is."

"Good.

"Now for the part that relates to peace.

"We, having been defined as separate through our creation, are then called to experience union with all that *IS*. And it is that process of experiencing union between your realm and my realm that will bring the peace you are seeking."

"How will that bring peace?"

"It will bring peace because union is peace. It is the failure to recognize union that creates conflict. We have peace in our realm because we are all Beings of Light and we know that we are all part of the Spirit. In your realm differences are perceived to be important. Your whole system of values is based on differences and you judge some differences to be more important than other differences. We know that differences are not important, in the sense that nothing is better than anything else. Enjoying difference is not a problem but valuing difference, thinking that difference is important, is a problem because that generates conflict. You see, difference is not difference. Difference is part of the same. All things and all beings are part of the whole. No part of the whole is any more important than any other part of the whole. Your realm is different from our realm, but it is not better than our realm nor is our realm better than yours. The realms are different, but they are both expressions of the same Spirit."

"But if you don't mind me saying so, Azar, this all seems rather simplistic. You seem to be telling me that if we all just recognize that we are part of the whole then everything will be fine and there will be peace in my realm."

"That is what I am saying, but that does not mean that it is easy to do. Principles that seem complex are usually much easier to follow than principles that are by nature very simple. It is doing that which is simple that usually causes one to become different. Creation comes out of simplicity. And what I am suggesting will require you to create that which has already been created. We, in this realm, call that Second Order Creation.

"We experience Second Order Creation when we choose to create something to be the way that it was originally created by the Spirit. That is quite difficult to achieve and requires that one truly align oneself with the will of the Spirit. In your realm you generally distort that which the Spirit has created. Instead of truly creating anew, you simply distort that which already *IS* into having the outer appearance of the original creation but not the true character of the original creation.

"The Spirit originally brought forth your realm in a state

of peace. You say that you value peace and wish to return to it. But you do not create peace. Instead, often through winning a war, you achieve a brief period with a cessation of fighting and call it peace. That is not peace. You have not created peace anew; you have not achieved a Second Order Creation of peace; you have only paused between states of war. In fact, it could be said that you are in a constant state of war because during those pauses that you call peace you continue to make preparations to defend yourselves in your next war. You cannot create true peace at the same time that you are preparing for war. That is why to truly create peace you must allow yourselves to be vulnerable."

"But Azar, if peace is not the absence of war what is it?"

"Peace is living in a state of harmony with the Spirit and with all of creation. It comes forth out of the simple recognition that all that *IS* is part of the whole. Difference becomes enjoyable, but unimportant, and conflict ceases. The absence of conflict is not peace itself, but it is a byproduct of peace. Recognizing the unity of all things is the key to achieving a Second Order Creation of peace."

"If it is really that simple, why is it so difficult?"

"Because to truly experience the unity requires giving up most of the distortions that you have made in other aspects of the Spirit's creation. It means giving up the illusion that difference is important. It means giving up the illusion that those who are different are the enemy. It means coming to the realization that it is one's own destructive nature that is to be feared and it means trusting that only through vulnerability can peace be achieved."

"You keep saying that it is necessary to become vulnerable. I still don't understand why that is necessary."

"I will only give you a partial answer at this point. My primary task now is to teach you about our realm because you must get to know us and to understand us as part of the process of establishing a linkage between your realm and ours. That linkage is part of the path to peace.

"Vulnerability is necessary because only through vulnerability can you deal directly with your own fear of losing control. To follow the path of peace one must totally give up the need to control others and give up the need to control events. When one gives up trying to control other's aggression, one is free to clearly deal with the aggression that lies within oneself. When one gives up trying to control events, one is free to deal with events the way the Spirit presents them. True peace is created within. As long as one is trying to create outer peace through controlling the aggression of others, or by controlling outer events, the pathway to inner peace is blocked. I have said enough about that for now.

"Are you getting tired yet?"

"No, I think I can stay a little longer."

"Good. There is a little more I wish to tell you before we stop for today.

"Communication between your realm and our realm can occur quite easily, but most people in your realm seem to be unaware of that. Deliberate communication like you are engaging in with me now is quite rare.

"We seek communication with your realm. We know that more communication must occur if our realms are to be linked. Strangely enough, many religious people seem to fear us and discourage communication with us. They proclaim that one should deal directly with the Spirit and that to communicate with other realms is evil. We find that logic to be preposterous. One of the functions the Spirit has assigned to us is to establish communication with your realm and to convey information to you in a form that you can understand and utilize.

"Those who most adamantly proclaim that they are in direct communication with the Spirit are not only arrogant, they are usually quite wrong. Some of them are in fact in communication only with their own prejudices and belief systems. Others are in indirect contact with the Spirit but assume that they are in direct contact. They fail to recognize that we are serving as intermediaries for the communication. Those in your realm are rarely in direct contact with the Spirit. In those rare situations where direct communication does occur, the recipient is usually totally surprised and overwhelmed by the experience. The Spirit is constantly creating, constantly bringing forth that which is new out of that which already *IS*. That is the Spirit's nature. Those who find the Spirit to be quite consistent and predictable are not in direct contact with the Spirit.

"Our role, in part, is to be of assistance to those who cannot tolerate the constantly changing nature of the Spirit and would be overwhelmed by a direct encounter. Our function is to temper the amount of information one receives from the Spirit. We serve as messengers with the capability of condensing and restricting the amount of information that is delivered to an individual. Most humans do not understand how truly overwhelming a direct encounter with the Spirit can be. We relay information. We filter it and reduce it to levels that can be tolerated. In that sense, we protect you from the Spirit, but we also make communication possible for all those who are not able to handle a direct encounter.

"Now the thing that can be quite confusing is that part of our function is to protect you from encounters with the Spirit, but we and you are also part of the Spirit. The ways in which we are the Spirit and the ways in which we are not the Spirit are part of the mystery of the universe. I cannot fully explain it to you because I do not fully understand it myself. You and I are part of the Spirit, but the Spirit is totally other than us also. The Spirit is constantly creating and changing but constantly remains the same. In our realm we have deep discussions about these subjects. We meditate about them with great regularity but none of us have total clarity about them. We, like you, pray to the Spirit. We pray to that which is other than us and yet we pray in the awareness that we are part of the Spirit and that we, like you, are moving toward total union with the Spirit.

"It is not that the Spirit is confused or that there is a lack of clarity about this in the mind of the Spirit. Our teachers are quite clear about that. Part of the mystery of the universe is found in the unfolding nature of the Spirit that is both in us and yet totally beyond us simultaneously. Some of our teachers suggest that in order to fully understand the mystery, one has to operate within the limitations of time such as you have in your realm. They say that we have difficulty understanding because we experience what we are and what we are becoming simultaneously.

"Or to put it another way, in the context of time, we are becoming reunited with the Spirit. We experience ourselves as being part of the Spirit, but we are not yet reunited with the Spirit, so we experience the Spirit as being other than us. But other teachers point out that beings in your realm, where time does exist, experience the same dichotomy that we do. They argue that since the problem exists for those who operate within the time dimension also, there must be some other principle, as yet undisclosed to us, that would account for this phenomenon.

"Jonathan, is it true that those in your realm experience both unity with, and separateness from, the Spirit?"

"Yes."

"I was afraid of that. This whole issue remains a mystery then. I am troubled by that which I do not understand. And I do not understand the Spirit."

"Perhaps the Spirit is not encountered through the understanding," replied Jonathan.

Azar paused. He pulsated for a moment and then said, "This is truly amazing! Our teachers have been saying the same thing to me. They say that I try to understand everything and that the Spirit cannot be grasped in that way.

Did they tell you to say that to me?"

"No. I've never met your teachers, at least not knowingly. What I just said is a widely known principle in our realm among those who follow the spiritual path. I am surprised that everyone in your realm is not aware of that principle."

"Why do you say that?"

"Because you are spiritual beings. You live in a closer relationship to the Spirit than we do, and you don't have the kind of limitations that we have in our realm."

"You seem to misunderstand something quite important, Jonathan. Our realm is not better than your realm. There are some things that we know about the Spirit from our experience, or from our teachers, that you do not know. But there is much that we can learn from your realm. We are not superior to you. A common misconception in your realm is that angels are all superior beings and that we have full knowledge of the Spirit. That is not the case. We are not by nature superior to you. We are merely different from you. Often what we are asked to relay to those in your realm goes beyond our own knowledge. We learn from what the Spirit says to you. The joining of our two realms is not merely for your benefit. We have much to gain from it as well."

"I'm amazed, Azar. I always assumed that Beings of Light were far more advanced than those in my realm."

"Well now you know the truth. We, too, work on our issues of spiritual development. Some Beings here are very advanced and serve as our teachers. But many of us are struggling along our path trying to reach clarity, just as you are struggling along your path.

"But we may need to stop here for today. You look very tired now."

"Yes, I am."

"We will stop then. There is no value in going beyond your limits. We will talk more in a few days."

Without further comment Azar faded away.

CHAPTER 4

Four days later Jonathan returned to the Realm of Light. Azar was waiting at the Portal as usual.

"Jonathan, I am glad to see you again," he said. "There is much that I want to tell you, but I am aware that you may have some questions. I want to give you an opportunity to ask them before we proceed."

"That is very considerate, Azar. I have been thinking a great deal about what you have told me so far and I do have some questions.

"As I understand it, the Spirit has ordained that your realm and my realm must come into an alliance, a partial merger, and that out of that merger will come the possibility of peace on earth. Is that right?"

"Yes, that is correct," said Azar pulsing with excitement. "Please go on."

"If that is the case, why is it that the Spirit has not revealed that plan to those in my realm?"

"Oh, but the Spirit has! It has been revealed to many of your more spiritual beings. Some have written about it, but their writings have been largely ignored. In fact, most of the religions in your realm address the coming merger in some way."

"Azar, I was raised as a Christian. I don't remember being taught anything in Christianity about a merger of the realms."

"If you look, Jonathan, you will find references to it in Christianity. Your realm has not been ready for the merger, so those references have usually been ignored or taken symbolically, but I assure you that they are there. The prayer Jesus taught his followers includes the words, "Thy kingdom come on earth as it is in Heaven." In Christianity there are many prophecies about the coming of a new heaven and a new earth, about a heavenly city made of light and about a reign of peace on earth. And much of the power that is potentially available in the Eucharist comes from the intersection of the physical realm with our realm. The bread and wine, which are physical, take on spiritual characteristics from our realm and become the body and blood of the Christ. That Eucharistic action brings the realms in close contact with each other. Christians don't seem to understand that anymore, but they used to. In the early days of Christianity people were willing to risk their lives to have an encounter with our realm through the Eucharist. Now Christians only seem concerned about their own physical realm. They ignore us and, largely because of that, their religious services are no longer empowering.

"Other religions have prophecies about the coming merger also. Look for them in their references to light and to peace. You will find them.

"Part of our mission here is to prepare those in your realm for the merger. That is not an easy task. Despite all major religions having references to us in their writings, people rarely pay attention to us or request our assistance. We know that there will be a great surge of interest in us when your realm is ready to sincerely pursue the path of peace, but that has not happened yet. We are hoping that your coming to our realm may be a sign that the focus is shifting and that humans are more open to interaction with us now.

"Those humans who are able to go to other realms usually go elsewhere for their instruction, even though we are available and frequently, without their knowledge, have assisted them in their work. There seems to be great resistance to the merger of our realms and resistance to encountering us directly. You are an exception. You found your own way to us. We are prepared to work with you and to share our knowledge with you."

"Azar, you say that peace will come about from the merger of our realms. But I still don't understand exactly how that will happen."

"It's complicated and there is no easy way to explain it to you. But I can tell you that after people become fully aware of their relatedness to us, they will become open to recognizing their relatedness to each other. That will lead to their discovery of the unity of all that is."

"But why should that be necessary? Why can't humans just recognize their unity with other people and proceed to make peace?"

"We too are puzzled by that, Jonathan. I do not have an answer for you. We know that vulnerability is essential if one is to achieve peace, but we lack clarity about why it is that people cannot make peace with each other until they have made peace with us. We only know that it is so and that the Spirit has instructed us to continue pursuing a relationship with your realm until the merger is achieved. I realize that this does not make logical sense to you now. I can only assure you that what I am telling you is the truth and that we are available to make the merger just as soon as those in your realm are willing for it to occur.

"Jonathan, up to this point I think I have done quite well in keeping my self-centeredness in check and in making way for your questions, but I am quite anxious to proceed with a new area of instruction. If you are willing, I will proceed. You can ask more questions later."

"O.K., Azar. I'm still confused, but my other questions can wait."

"Good, Jonathan. I want to see if our assessment of the

inner nature of beings from your realm is correct. You must realize that all of our knowledge about you and your realm comes from what little the Spirit has revealed to us and from the reports of those who have been given assignments in your realm. We have made a number of observations, but we have rarely had an opportunity to discuss our conclusions with a human. I, myself, have been particularly interested in collecting information about your realm and about human beings in particular. I would very much like to discuss my conclusions with you. Is that acceptable to you?"

"Yes."

"Good." Azar started pulsing rapidly. "You don't know how exciting this is!

"Well, first of all, we have noticed that there is much talk about love in your realm but there appears to be very little practice of deep love for each other or for the Spirit. It is clear to us that those in your realm are much more interested in ideas than in actions. Some of us here have suggested that for humans talking about something has the same value as doing it. Is that correct?"

"No, Azar, actions are important. It is through actions that the sincerity of the talk is demonstrated."

"Really? If that is the case why is it that your religions seem to be practiced primarily through talk rather than action?"

"I don't know, Azar. I guess because it's easier to talk about principles than it is to practice them."

"Really? Do you mean that some in your realm use religion as a way to avoid real growth?"

"It certainly seems that way, Azar."

"Then what is the purpose of your religions? I don't understand."

"Many believe that religions help us relate to each other and to the Spirit."

"But, Jonathan, even in your realm the Spirit is

everywhere and in everything. How can you not relate to the Spirit?"

"Well, I guess you have a point, Azar. Many people think that they must do particular things and believe certain things in order to be in a relationship with the Spirit. They follow certain practices including prayer and worship services in order to deepen their relationship with the Spirit."

"I can understand the value of communicating with the Spirit and worshiping that which *IS*. We do that also. But I don't understand how one can deepen a relationship that is already complete."

"Azar, many humans do not experience their relationship with the Spirit as being complete."

"How could it not be complete? I find your religions very strange. How could the Spirit that is, be anything other than what is, and how could one relate to that which is complete and experience it as incomplete? One relates to the Spirit. There is no way not to relate to the Spirit. And when one relates to the Spirit it is complete. How could it not be complete?"

Azar's luminescence became dimmer as he pondered these issues. Then it suddenly brightened again.

"I have it!" he said. "Those who experience incompleteness are not worshiping the Spirit! They are worshiping their projection of what they think the Spirit is. There is no other explanation! They experience their relationship with the Spirit as incomplete because their projection is a distortion of reality. Projections are not First or Second Order Creations; they are always distortions of what is. If your beings were relating to their projection of the Spirit they could, in fact, experience the relationship as being incomplete. Now it all makes sense. Tell me, is the experience of incompleteness that you mentioned rather rare among your beings, or is it common?"

"Most humans experience incompleteness in their

relationship with the Spirit."

"There you have it! Your religions pursue projections of the Spirit rather than the true nature of the Spirit. That explains our discomfort."

"What discomfort, Azar?"

"On some occasions, Beings of Light do still attend religious observances in your realm. They almost always report feeling very uncomfortable there and they usually return drained of energy. Since we have no religions here, I had assumed that they find themselves drained because they are dealing with something unfamiliar. That explanation never made much sense to me, especially since I am told that there are a few churches and other places of worship where angels do feel welcome and genuinely enjoy their visits. Those exceptions do exist, but by and large, we prefer to avoid churches and religious ceremonies in your realm.

"Many things in your realm are strange to us. We do not have physical bodies as you do, so sexual expression is totally foreign to us. We do not have physical possessions. Money and ownership are quite foreign concepts to us. War seems strange to us and moving your enemies to another realm through killing them seems ludicrous to us. The list of differences is almost infinite, but what troubles us most is your religious practices. Why should that be? I think I finally have the answer. If you don't mind, I will discuss my insight with some of our teachers."

Before Jonathan could respond, Azar disappeared from view. Then he reappeared almost immediately.

"Forgive me for not inviting you along, Jonathan, but I thought it inappropriate at this point for you to be present. I assumed that our teachers might find it awkward to openly discuss these issues with you present. Sometimes they make reference to deep knowledge that has not yet been given to your realm by the Spirit. If that were to occur it could result in much confusion for you. I did not want to run that risk.

"The discussion was quite interesting. In a way, I wish you could have been present for parts of it. I will share a portion of it with you, if you like."

"Yes, I would like that very much."

"The conclusion they came to was that I was indeed basically correct in my assessment. They did, however, say something that might be of interest to you, if you are not already aware of it. They told me that part of the evolution of your realm is movement toward people developing the ability to worship in spirit and in truth. That ability is incomplete for most beings currently in your realm, but when the evolution is more complete, religions will cease and all in your realm will encounter the Spirit directly, as we do. Then it will no longer be necessary for us to serve as mediators between beings in your realm and the Spirit. I did not know that was part of the Spirit's plan. Your realm is moving toward that, but it will not be achieved until after the merger has come to pass."

"Azar, there are some in our realm who proclaim that we already worship in spirit and in truth."

"They are incorrect. Your realm is moving toward that state, but it has not yet been achieved. Our teachers agreed that, at present, most of the worship that occurs in your realm is worship of your own projections of the Spirit. After the merger, religions will cease, and you will live in harmony not only with all those in your own realm but with us as well. We will be welcomed to participate in your activities, and we will no longer hide ourselves from view. In addition to being able to experience time whenever we like, we, Beings of Light, will experience a great period of learning and realms that have been closed to us will be available for the first time."

"What realms are closed to you now?"

"I cannot answer your question for two reasons. First, the Spirit has not yet revealed the existence of those dimensions to those in your realm. If I were to reveal their existence to you now it could cause you tremendous confusion. I do not wish to do you harm. But second, even if I were allowed to describe the characteristics of those dimensions to you, I could not. There is no way to put such a description into terms you could understand. I cannot describe things that are so dissimilar to everything you have previously encountered. The descriptions would have no meaning to you. Descriptions are only of value if comparisons can be made with things that are already familiar. There is almost nothing in those realms that is similar to what you have already experienced."

"Azar, if you haven't experienced those realms how do you know they exist?"

"The Spirit has revealed their existence to us, just as the Spirit has chosen to reveal the existence of our realm to those in your realm."

"In what ways has the Spirit revealed the existence of your realm to us?"

"There are many brief references to us in your scriptures and, if one searches for them, one can find longer descriptions of our realm in books written by a few people who, like yourself, have journeyed to our realm. All of those descriptions are superficial and cannot give humans a real sense of what it is like to exist in our realm, but the descriptions are there nonetheless and beings from your realm can read them if they like."

"Azar, how did your teachers find out about those other dimensions that you mentioned? Did the Spirit tell them directly?"

"Yes, but we have also had occasional visitations from beings who have come to us from those other dimensions. They try to tell us what their dimensions are like, but there is little we can understand from their reports. They do inform us that to exist in their realms is wonderful. I long for the clarity that would enable me to enter those other dimensions."

"How many dimensions are there?"

"I am not free to answer that. But I can tell you that existence goes very far beyond the number of realms that are currently open to beings from your realm."

"How many are open to beings from my realm now?"

"There are seven, six besides my realm. It is possible for spiritually advanced beings from your realm to travel to any of the seven. The others are not available."

"Have all of the seven realms been visited by beings from my realm, Azar?"

"Oh yes, but those visits are quite rare. It is not easy to move through the boundaries between your realm and those seven other realms. Most humans are not capable of doing that. But those realms are not closed and more spiritual beings, like you, can go to them."

"I would like to hear more but I am growing very tired. I think I need to return to my own realm now."

Azar looked intently at Jonathan. "Yes, you must go. Do not delay. We will talk more the next time you come."

Azar disappeared.

Jonathan quickly proceeded to the Portal and returned to his own realm.

CHAPTER 5

On his next visit, after greeting Azar, Jonathan opened the discussion. "Azar, there is something that has been bothering me for a while, but I have been reluctant to tell you about it."

"What is it Jonathan?"

"Well, Azar, I'm not quite sure how to say this. It's not that I mind coming to your realm. In fact, I look forward to my visits here. It's something else."

"Yes, Jonathan, go on."

"Azar, the Beings I met the first time I came here said they wanted me to teach others about what I learn from you. It's that part, Azar. It's the part about teaching others. I don't really enjoy teaching. I have always liked learning but for some reason I have never really enjoyed instructing other people."

"Are you willing to teach?"

"Yes. In fact, that's part of my work now. I share wisdom and knowledge with people in order to help them solve their problems. But there are some people who seem to enjoy the sharing of knowledge far more than I do."

"Jonathan, I do not have clarity about what you are saying to me."

"The problem is, Azar, I'm not sure I am really called by the Spirit to teach."

"I still do not have clarity, Jonathan. You say you are

willing to teach. What is the problem?"

"There are people who enjoy teaching. I teach but I don't like to teach, Azar. How could the Spirit be calling me to do something that I don't like to do?"

"Jonathan, both in your realm and mine, the Spirit quite frequently calls a being to do work that the being does not enjoy. The calling does not come out of the being's own desire. The calling comes out of the Spirit's desire. You happen to resist your calling to teach others. That does not matter. That you do not like it does not mean that you are not called to that work. The important thing is that you accept your calling and that you continue to grow while you are doing that work. The Spirit wants you to grow. It is out of kindness that the Spirit has called you to teach. Although you might enjoy some other type of work more, you would not grow as much if you were doing something else. If you continue to grow, you may come to love doing that which you do not enjoy now. Or, if you continue to grow, you may eventually be called to do a different task that you might enjoy more than teaching. Growth is the key. Do not judge the validity of your calling by how much you enjoy it. Not everything that is important is enjoyable."

"I will think more about what you have just said, Azar. But there is another aspect of this issue that also confuses me. You said that Beings of Light are quite often involved with people in my realm. I have been wondering, why is it that you are instructing me here? Wouldn't it be more effective for you to convey your information to people in my realm directly, rather than using me as an intermediary for your information?"

"Jonathan, the answer to that is quite simple. We find it difficult to get across large amounts of information to most beings in your realm. Many of them are not actively seeking enlightenment. Others mix what comes from us with their own thoughts and fantasies. That's how we ended up with feathers."

"Feathers? What are you talking about, Azar?"

"I'm talking about feathers. Some artist or other in your realm learned that we have something *like* wings and decided on his own that we do have wings and started painting us with wings with bird feathers all over them. That's what I've heard. Some Beings here think that's funny. Well I don't think it's funny. I think it's disgusting!"

Jonathan noticed that Azar's luminescence had shifted to a reddish tint.

"OK, Azar, I didn't mean to upset you. Let's change the subject. Can you tell me about guardians? Do all humans have a guardian?"

The reddish hue faded.

"Yes, Jonathan. There are two kinds of guardians available. There is at least one guardian, and sometimes more, from our realm assigned to each person in your realm. The guardian's function is to help advise the individual with regard to spiritual issues, to translate information from the Spirit and to generally assist with issues of personal growth. Occasionally the guardian may serve in a rescue capacity by helping to maneuver events into more favorable patterns for that individual. When that occurs, it is quite often referred to as a 'miracle' by those in your realm. Actually, our preference is to work with issues in other ways than deliberately altering patterns of events. Whenever possible, we like to help individuals change their attitudes and thought processes to forms that naturally create more favorable outcomes. When that is not possible, we will sometimes intervene in ways that can appear quite dramatic to human observers. We have been known to affect what you call nature by stopping storms or bringing rain or even moving an individual from one location to another, but, as I said, we prefer to use other methods.

"Guardians are far more involved in your realm than most of you realize. I have never been assigned that function, but those who have, tell me that it is not an easy task. Beings from your realm can be quite obstinate. They have a tendency to create reality in ways that are destructive to themselves and they can be quite resistant to our guidance that could assist them in their personal growth. The other thing that makes our work difficult is that our presence is usually ignored, and we are rarely asked directly for assistance."

"Do I have a guardian?"

"Yes, of course. As a matter of fact, you were assigned three because of the special character of your work. But to have three is rare. Most have one. Occasionally two are assigned but only rarely are three provided.

"There is only one instance that I am aware of where an individual was assigned four guardians. He was a great religious teacher in your realm. He called heavily upon his guardians for wisdom and on a number of occasions he had to call on them to rescue him from some rather nasty scrapes he got into through sharing his wisdom with individuals who were not receptive to his teachings."

"Can you introduce me to my guardians?"

"Yes, but you don't need me for that. All you need to do is to ask them to reveal themselves to you. They would be delighted if you did that. It is far easier for guardians to work with individuals who are acquainted with them."

"Do they show themselves?"

"They might. Guardians can reveal themselves in a variety of ways. Some merely speak to their charges; others reveal themselves through appearing as a luminous presence like a cloud; others reveal themselves through a special feeling that their charges can sense. There are many ways and most guardians are quite willing to reveal themselves to those who ask."

"You said there are two types of guardians. Can you tell me about the other type?"

"No."

"Why not, Azar?"

"That information would not be useful to you."

"What about guides? Are guardians and guides the same?"

"No. Guides are usually beings from a different realm than ours. In most cases, they are beings who have existed in your realm previously. They seek to assist with problems and to give practical advice. There are exceptions, but generally guides are less concerned with spiritual issues than they are with physical reality and how to deal with it. Most guides liked their physical existence and enjoy the opportunity to vicariously participate in it again through their charges. It is important to know that guides usually volunteer and are not selected for their spiritual qualities. A frequent mistake made by some people is the practice of consulting their guides about matters that are essentially spiritual in nature. Guides do not necessarily have more wisdom in those areas than their charges. Consulting them as though they were experts can lead to problems. Some guides like to expound on their own religious theories and present them as though they are the truth. There are other types of beings, who are not guides, who will also rather freely share their ignorance and expound about subjects they actually know little about. Beings in some of the other realms are not necessarily more advanced than beings in your own realm. And beings that are contacted through table tapping, Ouija boards, and automatic writing are notorious for providing misinformation.

"That is not to say that all information received in that fashion will be incorrect nor that the beings contacted necessarily have malicious intent. The problem is that it is relatively easy for beings who have previously lived in your physical realm to communicate through table taps, Ouija boards, or moving a pencil held by a being still in the physical realm. Because it is so easy to do, beings with very little spiritual sophistication are capable of using those physical methods to communicate with beings in the physical realm. Be careful, many of them will try to communicate with you when they actually have little that is useful to contribute."

"What form of communication between realms can be trusted?"

"None."

"None?"

"Yes, none. There is no form of communication that is totally reliable. All forms are susceptible to abuse by beings with malicious intent. And all forms of communication can be misunderstood by the recipients at times. Furthermore, any form of communication can be used by some beings who have the best of intentions but communicate falsehoods because they are incomplete in their own understanding. In general though, the more sophisticated the form of communication, the more reliable it is likely to be. Thoughts of an inspirational nature are more often reliable than automatic writing and the other physical means I mentioned. Inspiration is the highest level of communication."

"What do you mean by inspiration?"

"Receiving information that is not in verbal form, a flash of insight or an understanding that must be translated into words or images by the recipient before it can be retained in the memory. Many artists, theorists, composers, and some writers in your realm operate out of inspiration. Some realize that their inspiration is coming to them from another realm, others don't. Occasionally inspiration may come through a guide or other being who is not functioning as a guide, but usually inspiration comes through one's guardian. Communication with the guardian can be enhanced by acknowledging the guardian's existence, by engaging in prayer, meditation, or focused solitude. Guardians communicate most clearly to those who provide spaces for communication to occur. Guardians report that it is difficult to communicate with charges who keep their minds cluttered with their own thoughts and concerns.

"Jonathan, we have been talking for quite a while. Are you tired?"

"I think I can stay a little longer, Azar."

"Good. There is a little more I wish to tell you about a subject we discussed earlier. It has to do with God.

"Beings of Light are generally, as I said before, rather uncomfortable at religious services in your realm. I wish to tell you more about that now.

"First of all, much of what beings in your realm attribute to acts of God or the Spirit, or whatever term they may use, are actually events orchestrated by us. And nearly all of the inspired messages that those in your realm receive come not directly from the Spirit, but through us acting as mediators. Now, in the larger sense, they are the Spirit's messages because they originate with the Spirit. But it makes us uncomfortable when people assume they are in direct communication with the Spirit when actually they are experiencing the Spirit through us.

"Most of the time we are not thanked for our role in what transpires. Although some thanks would be appreciated at times, it is not the absence of thanks that really bothers us. It is that we unwittingly find ourselves in the role of perpetuating the myth that people are having direct encounters with the Spirit. Beings in your realm almost never encounter the Spirit directly. The Spirit is too powerful, too awesome, too other than you, to behold directly. The Bible and other religious writings we are aware of make that clear with statements such as, 'No one can see the face of God and live.' People used to fear direct communication with the Spirit. They understood that it was dangerous.

"That principle was understood more clearly in earlier times than it seems to be now, and our role as messengers for the Spirit was more often recognized by humans in the past than it is now. We do not like to tacitly be promoting a falsehood and yet we do not wish to withdraw our help and support from beings in your realm who think they are communicating directly with the Spirit. At times it seems to us as though our communications and our actions are being worshiped instead of the Spirit, the true source behind our actions. We do not wish to be worshiped and we do not wish for our communications to be worshiped. To be acknowledged, appreciated, even thanked is fine but do not worship us. The Spirit is far more awesome than any of you can possibly imagine. Worship that which is beyond description. Do not worship us or our actions. We are merely a part of the Spirit's creation."

"I can understand your discomfort with the distortions currently being promoted by some in our religions. How can that be remedied?"

"The Spirit assures us that when the merger of our realms starts to take place, those in your realm will experience a surge of interest in us. Our function will become more clearly understood and a desire for more interaction with us will develop. It is possible that your arrival in our realm is a sign that the proper conditions for a merger are starting to unfold."

"Azar, I am becoming tired now. But there is one thing I am still confused about."

"Speak quickly."

"You talked about the Spirit being beyond anything people can imagine and that people rarely encounter the Spirit directly, but previously you said that we are all part of the Spirit. I don't understand."

"Jonathan, that is one of the great mysteries about the Spirit. I can explain it, but you will still be confused. In the realm of the Spirit opposites can be true at the same time and usually are. The part of you that has not merged with the Spirit experiences the Spirit as beyond anything that can be imagined. The part of you that is moving toward merging with the Spirit finds the Spirit within. Worshiping the Spirit 'in spirit and in truth' demands that both of those truths about the Spirit be encountered simultaneously.

"You must go. I can say no more at this time."

Azar was gone.

CHAPTER 6

The next evening, Jonathan passed through the Portal expecting to find Azar waiting for him as usual, but there was no one to greet him. He waited a while, but Azar did not appear. As he was puzzling about what to do next, Jonathan noticed some Beings of Light gliding along what appeared to be some sort of a path or roadway in the distance. He became intrigued by their activity and decided to explore it while he waited for the appearance of his luminous friend.

Jonathan visualized the road in his mind and instantly found himself standing in the middle of an absolutely straight thoroughfare that stretched as far as he could see in both directions. As he stood there, a Being glided toward him.

"I am looking for Azar," Jonathan said when the Being drew close.

"You will find him where he is in the *IS*," said the Being without slowing his pace.

"And where is that?" asked Jonathan.

"*IS* is always wherever *IS* is," replied the Being as he passed.

Jonathan pondered the peculiar response he had been given and then traveled down the road in search of Azar. He visualized himself moving along the roadway and instantly found himself gliding along without moving his legs just as the Beings of Light were doing. He discovered he could move quite rapidly or very slowly merely by thinking about traveling at a different speed. The Beings, however, were all traveling at about the same speed. Jonathan adjusted his rate of travel to match theirs and fell in at the end of the line and proceeded down the road with them.

"May I ask where you are headed?" Jonathan asked one of the Beings directly ahead of him.

"To the city," came the response. "To the city, but that is unimportant."

"And where are the Beings going who are headed in the opposite direction?"

"Away from the city," was the cryptic but courteous reply. "That too is unimportant."

Jonathan glided along in silence for a time and then noticed a Being standing beside the roadway in the distance. As he approached, he recognized that it was Azar and shot forward to join him.

"I thought it was time for you to experience a bit of our existence," said Azar. "How did you like your journey in our realm?"

"It was very pleasant," responded Jonathan.

"Do you have any questions?"

"Yes. I noticed that I could travel at any speed I chose and yet the Beings of Light were all traveling at about the same velocity. Why don't they travel faster?"

"Because they enjoy the view."

"What view?"

"You didn't see anything along the way?"

"No."

"I was afraid of that."

"Why, Azar, what was there to see? I saw a road with some Beings traveling along it. What else was there?"

"When you looked to either side of the road what did you see?"

"I saw light."

"Light?"

"Yes. Light. Everywhere I looked I saw light."

"And on your other visits here what have you seen?"

"I have seen you and some other Beings that are made of light."

"Nothing else?"

"No. Why? Is there something else to see?"

"Jonathan, I am afraid we have a great deal of work to do. I was assuming that you were experiencing what is here. Tell me, when you take a journey along a road in your realm what do you think about?"

"I think mostly about the place to which I am going and what I will do after I get there."

"You may be traveling, Jonathan, but that is not a journey. If you traveled like that in our realm you would instantly arrive at the place you thought of and there would be no journey."

"I don't understand."

"Jonathan, the journey is what you experience along the way. That is the value of the journey. If you arrive, you are no longer on a journey. To journey is to grow, to experience, to absorb into oneself all that is along the path. To arrive somewhere merely gives one the opportunity to experience what is available in that one, new, location. It is along the way that our true growth occurs and, if I am not mistaken, that same principle applies in your realm as well.

"We have been told that many humans do not understand how to take a journey. They think that arriving at the destination is what gives a journey its importance and we are told that they focus on the destination, just as you do. That is a terrible waste.

"You saw nothing on your journey today because you did not look for what is there. Like your realm, our realm is filled with beauty that surpasses all description, but it can only be beheld by those who look for it.

"Look around you now and tell me what you see."

Jonathan turned slowly around as he looked in all directions.

"I see light, lots of light, and I see the road with a number of Beings moving along it in both directions."

"Amazing! Absolutely amazing!" exclaimed Azar with a distinct tone of exasperation in his voice.

"Why? What more is there?"

"You don't see the hills and valleys, the trees and the meadows of flowers. You don't see the stream flowing down into the Crystal Sea?"

"No."

"No?" repeated Azar in disbelief. Then he started to laugh. There was a beautiful sound to his laughter, a light, lilting, musical quality that communicated a sense of deep joy to Jonathan.

"Your laughter, Azar. It's beautiful!"

"Yes it is," agreed Azar. "And the creation is beautiful. It sings with us when we laugh. Jonathan, you must laugh to see the beauty around you. You must come to realize that nothing in all creation is serious. It is all joyous. It is all to be experienced in beauty and in wonder.

"I was laughing because it all became clear to me. You don't see the beauty because you think that creation is serious and that your journey should be a serious task that requires focus and concentration. You don't see what's all around you because it would distract you from the seriousness of your task, getting to your destination. Don't you understand yet that you are always at your destination? *IS* is. *IS* is everywhere. Everywhere is filled with beauty and life. And the destination that you are so seriously pursuing is only one more point of *IS* in a creation that is all *IS*.

"Do you understand, Jonathan? The journey *IS*. *IS* is the journey and the journey is filled with joy because that is what joy is. Joy is being in touch with what *IS*. When one is in touch with what *IS*, every journey is filled with joy.

Even the journeys that lead through difficult experiences in the desert are joyous and filled with beauty. When one knows that the desert also is *IS*, then it too is filled with beauty.

"We are standing in a beautiful spot. The view is gorgeous. But then again, all of the views along the journey are beautiful in their own way. When one thinks that the destination is more important than any other point along the way, the beauty disappears and there is only the road to be followed.

"Look around you Jonathan. Look around you and see. This point in the journey *IS* and the view, as always, is spectacular. But once you see it do not linger. If you do, *IS* will become *WAS* and it will lose much or all of its beauty."

Jonathan looked again. Suddenly it was all there. He could see everything Azar had described and more. It was all there, and it had beauty beyond anything he had ever experienced before.

"I see it!" Jonathan exclaimed. "I see it and its spectacular!"

Azar laughed again, a laugh of joy and fulfillment.

"Good," said Azar. "Now you are learning to see. Don't linger here. We have covered enough for today. Journey back to the Portal and return to your realm. *IS* is there as well."

Jonathan followed Azar's directive. All along the way was ever-changing beauty. He passed through the Portal and returned to his own realm. It was the same as he remembered it. The same and yet forever different. It was all beautiful.

CHAPTER 7

The next time Jonathan returned to the Realm of Light, Azar
met him at the Portal.

"We have much to discuss today," Azar said. "We will
stay here, next to the Portal."

Jonathan was disappointed. "After what I saw last time
I had hoped that we might journey through more of your
realm. I have never seen such beauty."

"That is why we must stay here."

"I don't understand."

"The beauty. We must stay here because of the beauty.
You want the journey to be about the experience of beauty.
But the journey is not about beauty. The beauty is there. It
is all along the way for those on the journey but unless the
journey is about change there is no journey. Jonathan, you
do not wish to change. You merely wish to experience the
beauty."

"How do you know that about me?"

"It is always the case for those who truly behold the
beauty for the first time. They go through a period of
seeking the beauty. But if they do not rather quickly regain
their purpose and pursue growth instead, the beauty will
disappear, and they will no longer be able to experience it.

"You have beheld the beauty. Now you know it is there.
Search within yourself for those things that must be
changed and pursue them, or you will lose what you have

found. Beauty is found by those who are in search of something else. Beauty is along the path but is not itself the path.

"What do you wish to change, Jonathan? In what areas do you wish to grow?"

"When I first came here I wanted to find the path to peace."

"Then we must quickly return to that task or choose another."

"I wish to return to the journey for peace."

"Very well then, I will continue your instruction. In time you will need to learn more within your own realm. We will arrange that, but for now, there is more you can learn about it from me here.

"The first thing that you must know about peace is that it is not a destination. Like beauty, it is found along the path, but, unlike beauty, it is found by those who are seeking it."

"Azar, that sounds like a contradiction. If one is seeking peace is it not a destination?"

"No, it is not, but you will not fully understand the difference immediately. Peace is found in a different way than beauty. I will try to put this in terms more familiar to a being such as yourself who experiences time. You will find peace not *during* the journey but only *after* the journey. One finds peace only as one looks back. Beauty is found in the *IS*. Peace is found in the *WAS*."

"I don't understand."

"Of course you don't understand! That's why you are here isn't it, because you don't understand the way of peace? I am here to teach you about us and to start your instruction about the way of peace. Until you understand, you will not understand.

"Understanding is found in the *WAS*. Beauty is found in the *is*. You will not understand now. And you do not have to keep telling me that you do not understand. Jonathan, it is your search for understanding that prevents you from understanding.

"To find peace one must not be on the search for understanding but on the search for truth. Peace is found in the *WAS* of the encounter with truth. And don't bother to tell me that you don't understand that. I know you don't understand. It has not yet entered the *WAS*.

"Truth is the key to finding peace. But truth is not quite what many in your realm think it is. It is encountered on a level deeper than knowledge and is experienced, rather than grasped, by what you call the mind. Truth is found, not by looking for it directly, but by merely being open to an encounter with reality. And to encounter reality, one must be seeking the Spirit while being open to any response the Spirit might make.

"Many people block themselves from a true experience of the Spirit by holding too tightly to their own beliefs about how the Spirit will respond. Beliefs can become restrictive. Those who pride themselves on their understanding of the Spirit cannot encounter the Spirit anew because the Spirit is usually encountered in unexpected ways. When seeking the Spirit, one must put beliefs aside and be open to what *IS*, in whatever form the *IS* might take. The Spirit encounters us in the *IS*.

"The Spirit meets those in your realm through encounters with the truth. Truth is not understood as long as it *IS*. Or, to put it another way, while one is in the midst of an encounter with the truth, the truth cannot be understood. The truth can only be understood in the *WAS* of the encounter. In the *WAS*, truth can be understood and put into the level of understandings or beliefs. The problem is that many try to encounter the Spirit through their beliefs or in ways that are in keeping with their beliefs; by doing that they block themselves from a true encounter with the Spirit.

"It is quite common for humans to try to educate children into an encounter with the Spirit. They teach their children to believe certain things about the Spirit and then assume that their children know the Spirit. Children are quite capable of encountering the Spirit without understanding or beliefs. In fact, it is children's ability to encounter what *IS*, without beliefs, that makes them so open to the Spirit. The Christ taught that one must enter *The Kingdom* as a child, without beliefs and without understanding."

"Azar, if you don't mind my interrupting, what is *The Kingdom*?"

"You will learn about that in your own realm, Jonathan. For me to get into that now would be a waste of what you call time.

"Remember, beliefs are restrictions for the Spirit. Beliefs are useful for dealing with that which has happened, but beliefs are totally useless with regard to making one open to encounters with the Spirit in the present or the future. Those who hang onto their beliefs too tightly and value them too highly prevent themselves from encountering the Spirit anew. To worship the Spirit 'in spirit and in truth' is to experience the Spirit without going through one's own beliefs."

"Azar, I'm feeling overwhelmed! How can you expect me to grasp all that you are saying? It's too much and it's coming too fast for me to absorb it."

"Good. That's the way it should be. I must overwhelm your mind, or your spirit will not be open to what *IS*. You are trying to arrange what I am telling you into principles and concepts that enhance your present level of knowledge and that can be applied in ways similar to how you have dealt with the Spirit in the past. I wish to overwhelm you with information so you will not be able to absorb it all and can encounter the Spirit without the benefit of your understanding and your beliefs. Truth breaks in when the mind is confused or at rest. At rest is better, but confusion works nearly as well. Your mind is not at rest, so I am deliberately overwhelming you with truths. When you are confused, you are open to experiencing the truth without interference from your beliefs.

"Never try to understand when in the midst of an encounter with truth. When truth *IS*, it can only be encountered. When the encounter is over, then the truth can be understood.

"Do you understand that last part of what I just told you?"

"Yes, I understand the part about not trying to understand truth in the midst of an encounter with it. The rest is a jumble in my mind."

"Good. That is the way it should be.

"Now leave before you try to understand what I have told you. You are in danger of missing the truth by trying to understand it. Leave. Go back to your realm. Let the truth speak within you. Do not try to grasp it with your mind. The truth *IS*. The truth is not to be believed until it is *WAS*."

Azar shoved Jonathan on the chest, causing him to tumble backwards. A strange tingling sensation pulsed through Jonathan as he tumbled out through the Portal and as Azar faded from view.

CHAPTER 8

Jonathan tumbled out of control down a great swirling vortex. Images of events in his life passed through his mind interspersed with images of Azar shoving him through *The Portal.* The tingling sensation increased, and he began to throb at an ever-increasing rate. He seemed to be rushing through space or time or reality or some cosmic substance beyond knowing. There was a roar, more like a high-pitched scream, that kept building in intensity as he hurtled round and round, down into the abyss.

Suddenly the sound stopped.

The falling sensation ceased.

And there was a great calm.

It was as though he were floating in nothingness, floating without any connection to who he was or who he had been or who he would be. He simply existed in an instant of eternal now, caught up in the Creator's great expanse of all that *IS.*

He floated or existed in that state with no awareness of time.

And then it happened.

The Spirit spoke. The Spirit spoke and yet did not speak. The Spirit was all around Jonathan; the Spirit was within Jonathan; the Spirit was Jonathan. Jonathan was one with the Spirit. He experienced the truth and for that instant he knew he was whole.

The voice, the Spirit's voice?, Jonathan's voice?, spoke and said, "We have come to give life and we are one. The union *IS* but also is yet to be. Live out of the awareness that *IS* and *WILL BE* are the same and you will find life."

Jonathan felt a profound calm as though everything in the universe was hanging motionless.

Then, as if by some great explosion, Jonathan was forced up through the center of the vortex and ejected into his own realm.

Jonathan looked around him. He saw the familiar surroundings of his earthly existence and collapsed into a deep, dreamless sleep.

CHAPTER 9

Jonathan's thoughts were streaming forth as Azar listened patiently. "Last night, after you shoved me through *The Portal*, I had the most amazing experience. I encountered the truth. We are one with the Spirit! I experienced it. I entered *The Vortex* and I have returned knowing that we are one with the Spirit. We are already that which we are becoming! We are becoming one, but we are already one. I experienced it.

"Azar, the ancients were right when they said that no one returns from *The Vortex* alive. They were right. *NO ONE* does return from *The Vortex*, only the *WE* returns. The *WE* returns, and in the *WE* is the fulfillment of everything that will come to pass. Everything is available now. It is possible to live out of the union with the Spirit now. The Kingdom, whatever it is, must already be available too. It's available but can't be accessed without the experience of being one with the Spirit. The Kingdom emerges somehow from within."

"Jonathan, what you are communicating to me is a little muddled, if you don't mind my saying so, but it is essentially correct. *The Vortex* does bring death. When the *I* dies, it is absorbed by the Spirit; the *WE* emerges and oneness with the Spirit is encountered. Merely communicating that understanding to people in your realm will not transform them however. They must encounter the

Spirit first and experience the oneness first. Only then can true understanding come."

"But how can I help the others in my realm, Azar? I want everyone to experience what I have experienced."

"It is the coming merger of the realms that will bring the awareness of the oneness to your people, Jonathan. Work for the merger."

"But how, Azar?"

"I do not know. I am here to teach you about us and about peace. That is my assignment. There are aspects of the merger that I do not know about. I do know, however, that the merger will not come until those in your realm are open to it. Be open."

Azar faded into the background.

CHAPTER 10

The day dawned bright and clear over the eastern mountains. Jonathan engaged in his customary prayers and then started reviewing Azar's teachings in his mind. "I still do not understand about *The Kingdom*," he thought to himself. "I remember hearing references to it when I attended church as a child, but I didn't understand what it was then, and I don't understand it now."

"Many people do not understand their own religions," said Azar as he came into view. "Why should you be any different?"

"Azar!" exclaimed Jonathan. "What are you doing here?"

"You have come to my realm, Jonathan. I thought it was time I came to yours. Besides, what I want to teach you today is rather long and complicated. If we tried to cover the subject in a session in my realm you would get exhausted long before I was finished. So, it occurred to me, 'Why not have the lesson in his realm?' I asked permission and was told I could come as long as I did not tamper with your reality. 'No miracles,' they said. I protested, 'Why should I be restricted? Other Beings of Light are allowed to perform miracles in that realm. Why shouldn't I have the same privilege?' But do you know what they said? They said I was too focused on myself to use good judgment about what is truly needed in your realm. They said that I could come, that I could continue your instruction and that I could experience the restrictions of time. But no miracles! Now what do you think of that? I didn't know whether to be proud that I was given permission to come or insulted that my visit was restricted.

"Oh, I'm sorry. I am forgetting my manners. I'm not letting you say a word and I haven't even asked whether you mind my coming to you here or not.

"You know your realm is really interesting. The scenery here is not totally different from ours. The vegetation is different of course, and you don't have as many colors as we do and the views are not quite as spectacular, but if this view is representative, the scenery here is nice. This is really nice. I like it. I shall recommend coming to other Light Beings who haven't come here yet.

"Of course, they couldn't come without permission, but I shall encourage them to ask.

"I wonder if they will be restricted with regard to miracles. I don't know whether to be insulted or..."

"Azar!" broke in Jonathan.

"What?"

"You are doing it again!"

"Doing what again?"

"You are talking about yourself and asking questions without giving me a chance to say a word."

"Oh my! I do believe you are right. And I had been doing so well. On the last few visits from you I thought I handled myself rather well. I did allow you to talk on those visits didn't I?"

"Yes, you did."

"In my excitement about coming here I must have fallen back into my old patterns. I'm sorry. Will you forgive me?"

"Yes, of course. But this is a threat, Azar. If I can't say anything, I won't speak to you."

Azar looked confused. "If I don't allow you to say anything of course you won't speak to me. Why do you say that is a threat?"

"Forget it, Azar. It's a joke."

Azar still looked confused. "I don't understand your humor, Jonathan. Do others in your realm understand your humor?"

"Not usually, Azar, or if they do they don't think it's funny."

Azar looked even more perplexed. "How can humor not be funny? If it's not funny, it's not humor. Is it?"

"Unless it's my humor, Azar. Most people don't think my humor is funny. That's why it's funny."

"Jonathan, are all beings in your realm as strange as you are?"

"Yes, Azar. But the funny part is that most of them don't know they are strange. I know it, and now you know it; but they don't know it. And that's what makes it so funny."

"Well, Jonathan, I don't really see what's funny about that either, but you think it's funny so that makes you funny."

"I think you are beginning to get it, Azar."

"Good. Now, Jonathan, if you don't mind my changing the subject, I will ask again if you mind my visiting you in your realm? This time I'll wait for an answer." He paused.

"Yes. You are welcome here, Azar."

"Thank you, Jonathan.

"Do you wish me to continue with your instruction?"

"Yes, please do."

"Very well. I would like to look around some more, but I will wait until after we have talked. I believe you were wondering about *The Kingdom* when I made my appearance. Let's get back to that subject, shall we? You do not understand your own religion. You prayed many times as a child for *The Kingdom* to come on earth as it is in Heaven. Did you not?"

"Yes, that is part of a prayer my mother taught me. I prayed it every night until I got older and drifted away from the church."

"You prayed that prayer and asked for the coming of *The Kingdom,* but you didn't know what *The Kingdom* would be like, did you?"

"No. Adults seemed to think that the coming of *The Kingdom* would be a good thing but they never explained what it would be like."

"That's what I thought. Jonathan, they didn't know what the coming of *The Kingdom* would be like either. And they probably didn't realize that we Beings of Light would have an important role to play in its coming.

"A long time ago you met a man who could have told you a great deal about *The Kingdom.* He sensed that you were not ready to hear about it then, so he did not talk to you about it. He is still living, and we suggest that you speak with him soon. He can teach you some of what you need to know."

"But I don't know who you are talking about. What's his name? How will I find him, Azar?"

"Don't worry. You will find him. We will see to that."

"All right. But is there any more that you can teach me today?"

"Yes. As I told you before, peace does not come from your realm; it comes from ours. In order to experience true peace in your realm you must be in contact with us because one of our assigned functions is to guide those in your realm into the way of peace. The Spirit has given us that assignment. But what must be understood is that just as the merger with the Spirit is something which is coming and yet can be experienced now, so the partial merger of the realms that is coming can be experienced now.

"Peace will break forth upon you from our realm. We in turn will be able to experience the restrictions of time whenever we choose. After the partial merger, Beings of Light will be able to come and go between the realms more freely and we will allow ourselves to be seen more frequently by those in your realm. Those from your realm will be able to come to us at will and we will receive all who wish to learn from us. *The Reign of Peace* will begin because the unity of all beings with the Spirit will be experienced. As the experience of that truth moves from *IS* to *WAS*, peace will unfold. That has happened to you already has it not?"

"Yes, it has. I experienced *The Vortex* and discovered that I will be and thus already am one with the Spirit. But I'm still confused about something. You said that peace comes after the truth. How are the two connected?"

"You realize that what I am about to do is of no value don't you? There is no value in explaining the connection between truth and peace unless one has experienced truth first. Do not expect that others will find value in what I am about to tell you until they too have experienced the truth. I am explaining it to you because you have experienced the truth and are ready to move from *IS* to *WAS*.

"The experience of the truth brings about the possibility of peace as one moves to the *WAS* because in the *WAS* the truth *IS*."

"I don't understand."

"Of course you don't understand! Don't you understand? You don't understand. That's the whole point. That you don't understand is the point. It is in the not understanding that the truth remains in the *IS*. In order for the truth to remain in the *IS*, one must remain in the state of not understanding. Those who live in the *WAS* of peace are those who live in the *IS* of truth. That is the reality. In the *IS* of truth, the *WAS* of peace is possible. The *WAS IS* with regard to peace.

"Do you understand now?"

"No."

"The *WAS IS*. The WAS *IS*, is the way it is."

"Do you understand that?"

"I think so, kind of. You mean that peace is encountered through keeping the experience of truth in the experiential level. By not trying to understand the truth of being one with the Spirit it is possible to have the understanding of how to achieve peace."

"That's close. That's real close, Jonathan.

"By keeping the reality of the truth in the *IS*, by experiencing the oneness with the Spirit, but not trying to understand it, it becomes possible for the *WAS* to become *IS*, in that peace becomes understandable when one is experiencing the reality of being one with the Spirit. When you are one with the Spirit, being vulnerable is not a threat to your existence. When you are one with the Spirit, vulnerability is understood as not being vulnerable at all. When you are one with the spirit, it is possible to be vulnerable in your realm of existence without being vulnerable in the ultimate realm of existence at all. In the ultimate realm there is no threat to your existence because your existence, in the ultimate sense, is assured by your oneness with the Spirit. You are invulnerable because you are already one with the Spirit and threats to your existence in your realm are not actually threats to your existence at all. Your ultimate existence is assured out of your oneness with the Spirit."

"But, Azar, I still don't like the idea of putting myself in the position of allowing someone else to have the power to kill me, even though I realize that they would only have the power to move me from one realm to another."

"But it can not be against your will if you choose the path of vulnerability. You are vulnerable when you do not choose the path of vulnerability, for it is then that something can happen to you beyond your will. When you choose vulnerability, even the malicious actions of another person against you are a result of you having chosen to be vulnerable to them. And if you are in the *IS* of the truth of your oneness with the Spirit then nothing that happens to you is beyond the will of the Spirit nor can it threaten your oneness with the Spirit.

"Do you understand now?"

"Yes. But my oneness with the Spirit is now in the *WAS* for me."

"It is in the *WAS* but that makes it in the *IS* because it is in the *WAS.*"

"Now I'm really confused."

"The fact that you experienced the truth of your oneness with the Spirit as *IS* makes it *WAS*. Because it is now *WAS* it still *IS,* in that the reality of having encountered your unity with the Spirit gives you the capability of re-experiencing that which *WAS* as *IS*. You can reenter the awareness of your oneness with the Spirit by engaging in *remembrance* of that which *WAS*. If you do that, it will become *IS* again. That is what remembrance, as opposed to mere remembering, is all about. When one merely remembers one's own experience, or vicariously remembers an event in history that was experienced by others, the event remains in the *WAS*. When you remember that which was *IS* for you in a way that makes it *IS* once again, you have experienced remembrance rather than simply remembering. The two are similar in action but quite different in effect."

"What determines whether it will be remembrance or mere remembering?"

"You do, Jonathan. You do."

"But how?"

"By *willing* to re-encounter the truth, your remembering will become remembrance. But that can only happen to those who have truly experienced the reality of the truth on a previous occasion. The problem with many of the religions in your realm is that those who practice them assume that through understanding alone the truth can be made known. But the *WAS* can not become *IS* unless it has previously been *IS* for that being. The truth must first be encountered on the level of *IS*. There is no other way to engage the truth. Those who try to experience the truth through others' experience of the truth always fail.

"The truth comes to those who are open to experiencing it, but it only comes as *IS* and it only comes when it is presented by the Spirit. You cannot make the truth come to you. You can be open to experiencing the truth, but you cannot make it happen. But once you have experienced the truth of being one with the Spirit as *IS*, like you did in *The Vortex*, that truth will sooner or later become *WAS* for you. But it can return to being *IS* by you willing it to be *IS* again. You will to make the *WAS IS* through remembering that which has for you become *WAS*.

"Remembrance is remembering plus having the will to re-experience what has become *WAS* as *IS*. That is what the central ritual in Christianity is all about, Jonathan. You were exposed to Christianity as a child. So, let's talk about this principle from the perspective of that religion. Our teachers have told us that the Christian communion service is, at its core, about re-experiencing the reality of Christ in the midst of the gathered people. People first have to have experienced the presence of Christ as *IS*. Then over time, that experience of the presence will become *WAS* for them, something that they have experienced in the past. Then, through an act of will, those who experienced the presence of the Christ in the past can choose to re-experience that presence as *IS*. Remembrance is the process of changing the *WAS* to *IS*. But the rituals have no power for those who have not previously experienced the *IS*. Many in your realm practice the rituals as though their will alone brings the *IS*. That's why we don't like to attend religious services in your realm. They lack power. There is no *WAS* that is being transformed into *IS*.

"I realize that I have been repeating myself, but what I am telling you is very important, and it is essential that you understand it. When the *IS* becomes *WAS* for you, you must understand how to make it *IS* again. The truth can not be kept as *IS*. It can only be experienced as *IS* and then becomes past experience as *WAS* and then, through remembrance, become *IS* again over and over again."

"I finally understand."

"Good.

"Now, that your lesson for today is complete, I am quite anxious to see more of your realm. Jonathan, are you willing to show me around?"

"Yes. What do you want to see?"

"I want to see all of it."

"I can't do that."

"Why not? There is nothing in your realm that the Spirit has ordered Beings of Light be excluded from."

"It's not that, Azar. This is a big realm. There is not enough time to show you everything."

"Oh, of course. How could I have forgotten? You operate within time here, don't you?"

"Yes. I'm afraid you will have to choose something you want to see on this visit."

"Then take me to church."

"To church?"

"Yes, to church. As I told you, we Beings of Light rarely go to church services in your realm. I'm quite curious about what goes on there."

"Alright. There is one not far from here. I will take you."

Jonathan took Azar on a short walk to the church. Azar seemed fascinated by everything he saw along the way and made constant comments about the beauty of this or the odd shape of that.

Although Azar was fully visible to Jonathan, the people along the street seemed totally unaware of his presence and several walked right through him. Azar found that amusing and started deliberately stepping into the path of people on the street and then holding out his hands in a mock attempt to ward off the collision. After the person passed right through him and continued on their way Azar would turn around and say, "Excuse me!" to their back and laugh in that beautiful musical laugh of his. He was like a child with a new toy.

"I find your realm quite enjoyable," he said as they walked up the steps of the church.

The church was half full of people and the service was already in progress when they entered. Jonathan and Azar took a seat near the back.

For a while Azar sat and watched with fascination as the people said prayers and sang hymns. Jonathan thought the sermon was well delivered but rather shallow, like many other sermons he had heard during his youth. Azar listened intently without comment. At the Prayer of Consecration Azar got out of his pew and glided up to the altar and stood beside the Priest. As communion was being distributed, he stood solemnly behind the altar rail and watched the people intently as they came forward and received the bread and wine.

When the closing hymn started, Azar returned to the pew. "Let's go," he said to Jonathan."

"It's impolite to leave before the end of the service," Jonathan whispered.

"All right, I'll wait." Azar looked bored.

When the service ended a few minutes later, Azar sailed right through the choir members in the back of the church and out the door. Jonathan followed behind as best he could. He caught up with Azar on the steps of the church.

"Why do beings in your realm go to church?" Azar asked.

"I am told, to encounter the Spirit and to worship."

"But most of them don't do that. Among all those beings present, only three of them encountered the *IS*. The priest did not even seem to be aware of the power that could be available to him. He was thinking off and on throughout the service about some problem or other he was having with the Budget Committee.

"I wanted to cause some sort of miracle to happen just to shake them up. But I followed my orders. 'No miracles.'

"Are most of your churches like this one?"

"Azar, I may not be the best person to ask because I have only been to a limited number of them, but what you saw today seemed like an average church to me."

"I see why most Beings of Light choose to stay away from your churches. I feel drained by the experience.

"I must go, Jonathan.

"Thank you for showing me around. I really enjoyed that walk down the street. The whole experience here, except for the church, was quite pleasant.

"Next time we will meet in my realm. I will see you there."

As Azar faded from view, people continued to come out of the church, shook the priest's hand and told him how much they enjoyed his sermon.

Jonathan returned home without telling the priest his own thoughts about the performance.

CHAPTER 11

When Jonathan returned to the Realm of Light, Azar was waiting just inside the Portal.

"I have continued to be troubled by my experience at that church in your realm," Azar began. "I lack clarity about several things. Would you mind spending some of this session on my issues?"

"Of course not, but it was very considerate of you to ask my permission."

Azar glowed more brightly. "I have been working on trying to be more sensitive to others and their needs. Do you think I really am becoming more considerate?"

"Yes, definitely. I have noticed a big improvement since we first met."

Azar started to pulse. "Hearing that gives me great pleasure," he said. Then the pulsing stopped and his luminescence dimmed noticeably. He continued, "Now to get back to this issue of church. I was deeply puzzled by my experience there. Despite the fact that there was much outward prayer and much talk about God, I found that my energy was being drained. I do not understand what many beings in your realm find so attractive about participating in an experience that is so unhealthy for Beings from my realm. And why do they talk so much about subjects related to experiencing the *IS* when so few actually do experience it?"

"I don't think I can adequately answer those questions, Azar. It does not make sense to me either. I, too, often feel depressed and drained of energy when I attend most church services. Because of that, I usually choose to stay away from them."

"Perhaps I should consult our teachers about this."

"That is a good idea, Azar. I would be very interested in what they have to say about it."

"Please wait here," said Azar as he faded into the background. Almost immediately he reappeared, glowing more brightly.

"What did they say?" asked Jonathan.

"It was very interesting, but in order for you to understand what they said I must translate their response into your concepts of past, present and future." He paused a moment and then continued. "They said that what I experienced was quite common now but that it was not usually the case in the early days of that particular religion. Initially, Beings from our realm felt quite comfortable at the services because most of the people in attendance were there primarily to re-experience the *IS*. In those days, Beings of Light quite frequently requested, and were usually granted, permission to attend the services and to perform miracles. There was much talk at the services about the coming of *The Kingdom* and we had reason to believe that that religion would indeed fulfill its destiny and serve to hasten the merger of our two realms.

"With the passage of time, however, the focus gradually shifted away from re-experiencing the *IS* and focused on merely talking about the *WAS*. Great value was placed on understanding and people started merely telling their children about the *WAS* rather than stressing the importance of being open to an encounter with the *IS*. Some people even came to believe that one's inner openness to the *IS* was unimportant and that encounters with the Spirit would occur automatically if the right beliefs were held and the rituals were performed correctly. That caused much focus to be placed on the form of the rituals rather than the mystery of the *IS*.

"As a result, Beings from my realm increasingly felt drained of energy when they attended the services. More and more of us stayed away, but surprisingly, our presence did not seem to be missed. Miracles became rare because there were few of us present to perform them. But many of the clergy explained away the absence of miracles by saying that the age of miracles was past and that people should no longer expect them to occur. The church continued to place its primary focus on the *WAS* and encounters with the *IS* became rare. Some of the liturgies did continue to formally mention us, usually using the word 'angels,' and in a few of the services they even requested our presence, but the clergy reading the liturgies usually had no real interest in us or our presence, so we rarely complied with their requests. Most of us have little interest in the church services now and are not willing to have our energy drained by attending.

"I don't want to leave you with the impression that we *never* come to services, however. Occasionally, a Being will volunteer to go and, on rare occasions, will even perform a miracle or two, but that is unusual. The number of Light Beings who still believe that the church has potential is extremely small, but that small group has been pushing hard for another attempt to infuse the church with energy from our realm. I have little hope that another infusion will bring about the merger because there have been a number of such attempts in the past that were unfruitful; miracles increased, power returned to the services, but each time those in your realm gradually lost interest in the *IS* and our attempts at bringing about a merger failed. After what I experienced at the service that I attended with you, I have no hope for the church. I have no hope, but our teachers keep telling us that the Spirit has not given up.

"That, by the way, is a characteristic of the Spirit. The Spirit does not give up even when I am convinced that the Spirit should. It is one of the things that I still do not understand about the Spirit. Not everything about the Spirit makes sense to me. In fact, most things about the Spirit don't make sense to me.

"My teachers have repeatedly told me that I follow the path of folly too much and that, just like your churches, I try to understand things before I experience them. That is a very disturbing thought for a Being of Light, but sometimes in my more enlightened moments I think they may be correct about me. They tell me to experience the *IS* of what they say to me. I do at times; I really do, but then I get so caught up in trying to understand the *IS* that it becomes *WAS*.

"As I talk about all this I have an uneasy feeling that my teachers may be right, that I am engaged in the same sort of process I find so disturbing about the people in your churches. I am starting to suspect that my teachers gave me permission to go to church in your realm because they thought I might come face to face with my own characteristics.

"Oh my, Jonathan, I just realized that I have been rambling on and once again have managed to turn our discussion into a monologue about me and my ideas. How can I ever get over this preoccupation I have with myself?"

"Maybe you just need to experience the *IS* of being you instead of the *WAS*. Is not the search for the Spirit the search for the *IS* of ourselves?"

Azar started pulsing rapidly. "Jonathan, that is profound. That's really profound."

"Just don't start thinking too much about it or you will have to start saying 'that was profound.'"

"That too is profound, Jonathan."

"Maybe it is, Azar, and maybe it just *IS*."

"Jonathan, you amaze me. How did you learn to think like that?"

"I learned it from you, Azar."

"Jonathan, I am learning from that which I taught you and in so doing it is becoming *IS* for me again."

"It is becoming *IS* for both of us, Azar. Perhaps that's what true learning is, encountering the *IS*."

"Perhaps so, Jonathan. On the other hand, if the learning is truly in the *IS,* then it is not in the *WAS,* and therefore can not be understood."

"That's true, Azar. Perhaps true learning never is understood and just remains in the *IS*."

"In that case, Jonathan, what is taught never is the truth. It only points toward the truth which remains in the *IS*."

"Does that mean that an encounter with the truth is also an encounter with the Spirit? Are the two the same, Azar?"

"I get the feeling that if we answer that question it will no longer be the truth."

"Perhaps so. Are you confused, Azar?"

"Utterly."

"So am I. But I think there is some *IS* in my confusion."

"I know there is in mine, Jonathan. I think we had better stop before we try to figure this all out and lose it."

"Agreed. Until next time...."

"Until next time."

Azar faded from view and Jonathan passed through *The Portal* confused but enlightened.

CHAPTER 12

On Jonathan's next visit, Azar met him with enthusiasm.

"Jonathan, I have continued to think about the experience I had in church and would like to ask you another question, if you don't mind."

"No, I don't mind. I might not know the answer, but I will tell you what I can. What's your question, Azar?"

"Do you remember I told you that only three people at the service experienced the *IS*?"

"Yes."

"I have been wondering what it was that allowed those three to experience the *IS* in the midst of an experience that was so draining for me and that did not bring an encounter of the *IS* to the others present. How did they find the *IS* during the service?"

"Well, Azar, I'm not sure I can answer that. I was raised in that religion as a child, but I have not practiced it for many years. As I remember, they emphasize having faith and then doing certain things like eating the bread and drinking the wine in that context. Although rituals make sense to me, I can't say that the one about bread and wine has ever had much power for me. Most of the people I knew didn't seem to experience much power in that service either. I'm afraid I can't be much help on this subject. Perhaps your teachers understand that religion better than I do, Azar."

"Do you mind if I consult them now, Jonathan?"

"No, not at all. I would like to know what they say."

"I will return," said Azar as he faded from view.

He was back almost instantly.

"They had quite a lot to say about the subject. I hope you did not have to wait too long.

"No. For me, you were only gone an instant.

"What did they say, Azar?"

"I am afraid that much of it had to do with concepts of physical reality that are familiar to us in this realm but would make little sense to you because they are quite different from the way those in your realm understand reality. Basically, they said that the ritual of the bread and wine is quite powerful and the reason few in your realm encounter its power is because they keep trying to understand it. They said that it is not a ritual of understanding and that all attempts to understand it stand in the way of experiencing it.

"They also said that for a period of time there was much focus in that religion on a debate between those who believed in transubstantiation as opposed to consubstantiation. Those terms have no meaning to me, but they said that you might be familiar with them.

"What do they mean?"

"Well, Azar, as I remember, they have to do with how the Christ spirit is present in the bread and the wine and whether or not the bread and wine are changed physically or just changed spiritually during the service. Beyond that I don't remember much about it."

"I see. Well, anyway, the teachers said that according to our understanding neither issue is of importance. They said that understanding the doctrine has little value and that the power of the ritual is not related to either concept. They said that the 'Christ spirit,' as you call it, is present in a far different way. It is not in the bread and the wine that the encounter takes place. It is in a dimension beyond your realm of reality or ours. They said that the bread and the wine are the portal into another realm of existence just as *The Portal of Light* is the portal giving you access to our realm of existence.

"The teachers said that Beings of Light have no access to the realm encountered through the portal of the bread and wine except through participating in the service with beings from your realm and passing through the portal together. Thus far that has not happened. We know little of the realm on the other side of the portal except that it will be accessible to us as a result of the merger of your realm and ours.

"I asked them why I had not learned of these teachings before and they said that they are teachings to be shared during the merger of your realm and our realm. I then said, if that were the case why were they sharing the teachings with me now? And then they said a strange thing. They said there are signs that the merger is starting to take place, but they said they are confused about something. They asked me about your profession. I said that you are a counselor of some sort. They asked me if I was sure. I said that you told me that you help people with problems and share insights with them. I told them that I think you are some sort of a psychologist or something. They told me to return and ask you again about your profession. That puzzles me, but I am doing what they asked.

"So, what is your profession, Jonathan? You are a psychologist, aren't you?"

"No, Azar. I am a shaman?"

"A shaman? Are you sure?"

"Yes, of course I'm sure."

"But you said you counsel people who have problems."

"I do. But I counsel with them as a shaman. I journey between the visible world and the spirit world to gain information and insights that I use to help people who are troubled."

"Jonathan, the information you have just given me may be important. Please wait here. I will return."

Azar disappeared again.

A moment later he returned.

"Jonathan, you have no idea how important that new information is! Do you know about the prophecy?"

"What prophecy, Azar?"

"It seems there is a prophecy in our realm that a shaman will come to us seeking peace when the merger is about to occur. The teachers had no idea that you are a shaman. They thought your coming to us had some importance simply because you were seeking peace. But until just now they did not realize that you are the shaman we have been awaiting. I can't tell you how excited they are. They are now sure that your coming to our realm is the sign indicating that the merger is almost at hand. They explained that my assignment as your guide is far more important than they had realized and that I am to play a significant part in the coming about of the merger.

"Jonathan, I was astounded. I had no idea that your coming to us was of such importance."

"Neither did I. I don't know what to say."

"The teachers said that we have been waiting for a being from your realm to come to us on a journey specifically seeking peace. Strange as it may seem, no one has come to us before to learn from us about the way of peace. A few have come with other issues or even out of curiosity, but you are the first to come on a quest for peace.

"The Spirit revealed to us that at the beginning of the period of the merger a shaman would come seeking peace. We thought that he would be seeking peace on his journey within our realm. It was not until I was talking to the teachers about the church service that they realized that your coming might have fulfilled part of the prophecy. Usually there is some sort of trick with regard to a prophecy, something that causes expectations to follow a different path than the one the Spirit actually plans to take. It prevents beings from forcing the prophesied events to unfold merely by their own efforts. The twist in this prophecy was the quest for peace. That the quest for peace might be a quest for peace within your own realm had not occurred to us. But the prophecy also stated quite clearly that the visitor to our realm would be a shaman. It was then that they told me to ask you more specifically about your profession. Now, we understand that you are the one who was coming. And through a strange twist of fate, I, with my problem of self-importance, accepted an assignment of importance far beyond anything I could imagine.

"This assignment is of ultimate importance and yet I took it without knowing that. I took it because others were not much interested in taking on an assignment of so little importance. I got the assignment because the teachers knew that I love an opportunity to expound on things I have learned and because no one else volunteered. My self-absorption led me to accept a holy mission without my knowledge of its importance. The merger of the realms is starting to unfold through us. Through us, Jonathan! Through us!"

"Are you sure about that, Azar?"

"Yes! And it is just the way the Spirit likes to work. The irony of it all! A third-rate 'angel' like me takes on a third-rate job as a tour guide for a being from another realm. No offense intended, you are not third rate, being a tour guide is third rate. And the third-rate angel takes the third-rate job because expounding on different issues makes the third-rate angel feel a little more important than third rate and thus he unknowingly accepts the most important assignment in the realm. I am truly humbled by all this. And all of this transpired while I was making rather fumbling attempts at trying to become humble.

"The Spirit has given to me that which I had finally come to desire. The Spirit has given me humility, Jonathan.

I'm no longer a pompous third-rate angel. Now I'm just an angel, an ordinary angel, and yet an angel with a first-class assignment. And the strangest thing in all of this is that the revelation we are dealing with here came about because I asked the teachers about that third-rate church service I attended. That service, too, is playing a part in all of this and will ultimately play a part in untold numbers of beings in your realm and in mine encountering and re-encountering the *IS!*

"And you, Jonathan, were unknowingly the messenger bringing the news that the era of the merger is finally at hand. Or, to put it another way, since you are functioning as a messenger to us, you are an 'angel' in our realm."

They both laughed. "You are the first person, I mean Being, who has ever called me that, Azar. But where are my wings?"

Azar laughed again and then became more serious. "I'm glad you brought that subject up, Jonathan. I have been meaning to ask you. How did beings in your realm ever get the ridiculous idea that we fly?"

"I don't know, but there are some references in our holy writings about angels having wings and I think some of them mention angels flying with them."

"It is incorrect to say that we fly. We don't actually fly in the sense that birds in your realm fly. When we choose to move from one place to another, but do not wish to arrive there instantaneously, we glide. It might appear as though we are flying but that is not actually the case. And to say that we have wings is totally false."

"Well what are those things coming out of your back?"

"These?" Azar said touching an oblong band of light emanating out of his back on each side. "These aren't wings. And we certainly don't use them to fly or even to glide."

"Well then, what are they?"

"These are bands of energy. They are expressions of who we are just like auras are bands of energy around beings in your realm."

"Oh.

"Well you must admit, Azar, that they do look a little like wings."

"Only to the uninformed, Jonathan, only to the uninformed."

"Well if they aren't really wings, why hasn't someone from your realm corrected our misconception before now?"

"I guess that the Beings who have been given assignments in your realm weren't as technical as I am and didn't think that it was important."

"I see. If you like, I will pass along the correct information about 'angel wings' when I instruct people about your realm."

"Good. I really wish you would.

"Now, Jonathan, to change the subject, I would like you to answer another question for me."

"Certainly, Azar, what is it?"

"What does ice cream taste like?"

"Ice cream?"

"Yes, ice cream. I have always wondered about that. A Being of Light who had been on assignment in your realm once told me that beings in your realm find great pleasure in consuming certain substances. We do not eat and we have no sense of taste. So, I would really like to know what it is like to eat ice cream."

"If you have never tasted anything, I don't know how to describe it to you. For me to say that it tastes sweet doesn't have any meaning to you, does it?"

"No. What is sweet?"

"I don't know how to describe it. Sweet is a taste that most humans find very pleasurable. Bitter is not pleasurable. Ice cream has a combination of a number of different tastes, sweet being the most predominant of them."

"I don't understand, Jonathan."

"I know, but I don't know any way to communicate it to you."

"Do you think, Jonathan, that after our realms are joined that I would be able to taste ice cream?"

"I don't know, Azar. But I hope so."

"I find it quite exciting to speculate about how the coming merger will affect us in this realm. Sex and ice cream. I have always wondered what it is like to experience sex and ice cream.

"Jonathan, you are beginning to look tired. I realize that it's time for you to go now but perhaps next time you can tell me what it is like to experience sex."

Jonathan laughed. "Azar, if describing ice cream is nearly impossible, describing sex is totally impossible. How can I possibly describe heaven to an angel?"

CHAPTER 13

Jonathan felt tired. He had been feeling too tired to journey to the Realm of Light for the past five nights. He thought about what he had learned on his journeys there. He meditated, rested, slept, met with friends for casual conversation. Nothing seemed to alleviate the fatigue he felt. Thoughts tumbled through his mind about the merger of the realms. Could it really be true that he and his friend, Azar, were involved in that great unfolding? Or was that merely some sort of strange fantasy he had dreamed up? Could his visits to the Realm of Light simply be in his imagination? He could not prove that he had been there.

Truths learned in his training came to mind. His teacher had said, "No shaman can prove the reality of the other realms. There are mere seekers of knowledge and there are true shamans. Many have glimpses into other dimensions of reality and experience things that cannot be proved or, in many cases, even described. However, the shaman visits other dimensions of reality, not for the experience itself, but to bring back knowledge for use in his own realm. The test of a true shaman is found in how effectively he can apply, in his own realm, the knowledge he has gained elsewhere."

Jonathan mused about the purpose of his journeys to the Realm of Light. He had gone to find the path of peace. Had he found anything that really would bring peace? Was the prophesied coming of *The Kingdom* really related to the merger of the realms? If so, why was that not stated more clearly in the holy writings? He thought about Jesus's prayer for *The Kingdom* to "come on earth as it is in heaven." Was that truly a reference to the merger of the realms? Could it be that one of Christianity's true missions is to propel the world toward a merger of the realms?

Jonathan suddenly remembered a monk he had met once many years ago at a monastery in the mountains. He had almost forgotten about him. Could this be the man that Azar had referred to? Jonathan remembered that he had stopped at the monastery when he was hiking. He had talked to the monk over a simple meal of bread and soup. The monk had asked Jonathan the nature of his occupation and when Jonathan had told him that he was a shaman, the monk had seemed pleased rather than dismayed. He then had said a strange thing to Jonathan. "One day my religion will be grateful to a shaman for opening the way to *The Kingdom*." When Jonathan had asked him to say more about that, the man had merely smiled and said, "Now is not the time."

Was that monk still alive? Would he be able to answer Jonathan's questions about the coming of the Kingdom?

Despite his fatigue, Jonathan decided to leave for the monastery.

CHAPTER 14

It was a long journey up the steep mountain path. The views along the trail were spectacular but Jonathan's fatigue made the trip an agony. He stopped many times along the way to rest. Pushing himself hard the last two miles, he reached the monastery shortly before darkness would have made the trail impossible. Daylight was rapidly fading when he entered the gate and knocked on the heavy wooden door of the large stone building. He could detect no sign of life as he waited at the entrance. The well-worn path leading to the door was the only indication that the building might still be occupied. Finally, he heard a bolt slide on the other side of the door and a young man wearing a thick brown robe stood facing him in the doorway.

"Peace be with you," said the young monk.

"And also with you," replied Jonathan and introduced himself. The young man listened but made no reply and did not introduce himself in return. Jonathan noted this lapse of etiquette but proceeded. He explained that he had come seeking a man he had met at the monastery nearly twenty years previously. He said the monk he was seeking was heavy set and of medium height, with an English accent and an unusually round face.

"From your description, that could be Francis," said the young man. "I believe he was with our order at the time of which you speak. He, like the others, has retired for the evening. Our life of prayer for the coming of *The Kingdom* demands that we rise before the sun. However, you may stay the night, if you wish, and speak with him in the morning."

"Thank you," said Jonathan, feeling relieved. "I am very tired from my journey."

"It is your quest for *The Kingdom* that is making you tired.

"Unless you insist on having something to eat, I will show you to your room."

"No. I brought some food with me and ate along the way."

"Good. Then come. I want to go to bed."

The rude little monk led the way down a narrow corridor lighted only by the lamp he carried. The lone sound Jonathan noticed, other than their own footsteps on the stone floor, was the muffled sound of snoring coming through a few of the closely spaced doors along the hallway.

"Our accommodations are simple, but I believe they will be adequate for your needs tonight," said the monk. He remained in the hallway as he ushered Jonathan through one of the doors near the end of the corridor. Jonathan entered a small room with barely enough floor space for him to stand after he placed the small pack he carried on the floor. The room contained only a bed, one chair, a chamber pot, and a small desk with a Bible, a prayer book, matches, and a candle holder on it. A simple wooden crucifix hung on the wall. The monk pulled a candle from somewhere underneath his robe, lit it from his lamp and placed it in the candle holder on the desk.

"I have been instructed to tell visitors to wake me if they need anything. My cell is directly across the hall from yours. Our first meal is two hours after sunrise. You may join us. The refectory, or perhaps you would call it the 'dining hall,' is down the hall and to the left. You will find it. May *The Kingdom* come soon."

Jonathan turned to thank the strange monk for his assistance, but the hall was already empty. He heard a thud as the door closed across the hall.

Jonathan undressed, climbed into bed and blew out the candle. The small room was plunged into total darkness. His weariness quickly overtook him, and Jonathan fell into a deep, exhausted sleep.

CHAPTER 15

He awoke with a start. For a moment Jonathan did not know where he was. He sat up, rubbed his face and eyes and tried to remember. Then it came back to him, the journey up the mountain, the peculiar young monk who greeted him at the front gate of the monastery and this small cell.

Guided only by the faint glow of the light coming from under the door, Jonathan found his clothes and dressed. Upon opening the door, he saw a great shaft of sunlight coming through the sole window at the eastern end of the corridor. He headed toward it, then turned left, as instructed, and found the refectory. The room had space to accommodate four or five times the present number of occupants. It was devoid of furniture except for a long wooden table and benches in the center of the room. As Jonathan entered, he counted a total of fourteen men standing along the sides of the table. The monks nodded, acknowledging his presence. The one who met him the night before said, "I see that you have found us. We are just about to have our morning meal. Sit there." The young monk pointed to one of the places already set with a fork, a plate, and cup. "We eat in silence," he added.

They all sat down at the table. The monks bowed their heads for at least a minute. Jonathan did the same. Then the monk sitting at the head of the table voiced a prayer.

"We thank you, O God, for providing us with the earth, the air, and the water; and for the sun which gives us life. May this food, which we are about to receive, give us nourishment to pursue our calling to hasten the coming of your Kingdom, through Jesus Christ our Lord." The others joined in voicing the Amen.

Then the meal began. One of the monks rose from the table and brought a pitcher of water and a pitcher of coffee from an adjoining room, which appeared to be the kitchen. After placing them on the table he returned to the kitchen and came back with a platter of scrambled eggs and dark, heavy bread which had already been sliced. The monks helped themselves to the food and ate in silence. Most of the men were well up in years. All wore the heavy brown robes of their order tied with a simple rope around the waist. Each man had hair that was cut short and all but four of them were clean-shaven. Despite the absence of conversation, they appeared to be a congenial group and Jonathan felt comfortable in their midst.

Jonathan surmised that the man at the head of the table was the abbot. Next to him was an elderly monk with a round face whom Jonathan thought might be the one he had spoken to years earlier. The man, not surprisingly, did not seem to recognize Jonathan when he had nodded to him before the meal, but he seemed pleasant and was welcoming of Jonathan's presence in their midst.

When all had finished eating, the abbot folded his hands in front of him. The others followed his lead and there was another period of silent prayer. Then the abbot voiced, "O Lord, as we continue the activities of this day, may we not forget that it is from you that we receive life and that it is to you that we shall return. Amen." The monks rose from the table and started taking their own dishes into the other room. Jonathan rose to do likewise. The men spoke softly to each other and some appeared to be joking with each other as they cleared the table. The monk that had met him the night before approached him and said, "We are allowed to speak if we wish for the next thirty minutes. After that we resume the silence and proceed with the work of the day. The man who sat to the left of our abbot is Francis, perhaps he is the one whom you seek." Before Jonathan could say, "Thank you," the young monk turned and walked away.

After the table was cleared Jonathan introduced himself to the other monks and found his way to Francis.

"My name is Jonathan," he said. "I believe I spoke to you many years ago when I was on a journey through these mountains. I have come to continue our conversation and to ask you some questions about *The Kingdom*."

"I am indeed pleased to have you with us," the monk responded. "My name is Francis. I have talked to many people over the years. Perhaps we have spoken before. Can you refresh my memory?"

"I am a shaman."

Francis raised his hand to his lips for a moment as he looked intently at Jonathan's face. Then there was a flash of recognition and Francis broke into a wide grin. "Yes," he said with enthusiasm. "Yes, I remember you now. You were hiking in the mountains. I met you on the East Trail. You asked me for directions. We got into a conversation and I invited you back to the monastery for lunch. You told me you were a shaman. I remember now."

"I have come back because you told me that one day a shaman would help to bring in *The Kingdom*. When I asked you for more information about that, you said it was not the right time to talk about it. I have returned with the hope that now is the right time.

"I have had some experiences in another realm, experiences that I find both meaningful and confusing. Although I have not continued on that path, I was raised as a Christian.

"Some of the things I was told in another realm about

The Kingdom are reminiscent of the teachings I received as a child. But I am confused. I'm not sure whether or not *The Kingdom* the Beings refer to is the same as the one spoken of in Christianity and I am puzzled by the prophecies regarding its coming.

"I am seeking answers to my questions and I thought you might be the one who could provide them."

"Jonathan, the coming of *The Kingdom* is indeed very close. It is now the time to talk openly about it. I will share with you what I know.

"The silence will begin again soon. I must get to my chores now. After lunch there will be another time for us to talk. Perhaps you can stay for a few days and we can pursue this matter in depth."

"I would like that."

"Good. Then we will talk after lunch. Our visitors are free to do as they choose the first day of their visit. After that, if they wish to stay longer, they are assigned chores and are expected to contribute to the life of our community.

"May I suggest that you use the time for a walk in the mountains? The view of the valley from the upper trail is truly spectacular this time of day."

"Thank you, Francis. Perhaps I will do that."

"It is good to meet you again, Jonathan. I look forward to our conversation this afternoon."

"So do I, Francis. So do I."

Francis smiled and nodded, then turned and left the refectory.

CHAPTER 16

Francis was indeed correct about the view from the upper trail. Jonathan found it magnificent. The sun felt warm on his skin and the air was invigorating. As he sat there absorbing the beauty of the scenery his strength gradually returned and his spirits lifted.

The sun was climbing high in the sky when Jonathan returned to the monastery. Since it was nearly time for lunch, he took his seat at the table and waited. Francis soon arrived, acknowledged Jonathan with a smile, and took his seat next to the abbot.

The meal began with a period of silent prayer followed by another prayer of thanks to the creator voiced by the abbot. It was a simple but tasty meal of hearty soup and bread. After the closing prayer the silence ended. Jonathan spoke briefly to the other monks and then joined Francis.

"Perhaps my cell would be a good place to talk," said Francis.

They left the refectory and walked halfway down the hallway to Francis' cell. The small room was identical to Jonathan's in every respect. Francis closed the door, offered Jonathan the only chair and sat down on the bed.

"I hope you don't mind meeting here," Francis said in a soft but still audible voice. "I wanted to meet in private because some of what I have to tell you might be troubling to the other monks. The redness of your face indicates that you have already gotten your share of sun for today and this is the only place inside that will assure we are not disturbed."

"It's fine to meet here," said Jonathan.

"First of all," Francis continued, "I want to say that I hope you have not been put off by your encounters with James."

"Oh, was that the young monk who met me at the door? He never told me his name."

"Yes, that was James. He means well, but he is not a very sociable fellow. He joined this order when he was only seventeen. He had a very deprived childhood and I'm afraid he has never really learned how to relate to other people."

"I did find him a bit strange, but I didn't take offense," said Jonathan.

"Good. He is really quite generous and a beautiful person, if you can ever get beyond his rather peculiar ways.

"Jonathan, I understood you to say that you are seeking knowledge about the coming of *The Kingdom*."

"Yes. As I said, I am a shaman. While on a journey in the Realm of Light I was told that peace can come only as a byproduct of a partial merger of that realm with ours. The Beings of Light referred to the coming of *The Kingdom*. I remember talk of the Kingdom of God in my religious education when I was a youth, but I don't remember getting any teachings about a merger between our realm and the Realm of Light. Can you help me to understand this? Does the coming of *The Kingdom* that is mentioned in Christianity have anything to do with a merger of two realms?"

Francis smiled. "You are the first person to ask me about the merger. I sensed that you might possibly be seeking information about that subject. That is why I suggested that we meet where our conversation will not run the risk of being overheard.

"I too have been to the Realm of Light. It first happened long ago quite by accident. I was deep in meditation when I saw an entranceway, or portal. I approached it not knowing where it might lead but decided, after some uncertainty, to enter it. I found myself immediately surrounded by white light of an intensity I had never experienced before. I encountered a Being who seemed to be made entirely of light. He told me not to be afraid and explained that I had come to the Realm of Light. That, I must say, was rather obvious," Francis said with a chuckle. "He asked me my purpose for coming. I told him that I had found the portal quite by accident during my mediation and had entered it out of curiosity. He told me that they were awaiting the arrival of a shaman on a mission of peace and that I was not to journey there again until after his arrival. He said that Beings of Light were available to me in my own realm, if I chose to receive them and that they would teach me about the coming of *The Kingdom*, if I wished to learn about it. I said that I would be most interested in learning about *The Kingdom* and would gratefully receive any Beings of Light that might be so kind as to visit me. The Being said that I was most courteous and that he would arrange for another Being to visit me forthwith. I must say that the whole experience was quite delightful. I have never been in any place where I felt such joy. I reluctantly followed the Being's request that I leave their realm. I returned to the portal and passed through it into my own realm again.

"I have not shared that experience with anyone until now. You are the first.

"A short while later," Francis continued, "a Being did appear to me in my sleep and told me that he had been assigned to me and that he would be available to instruct me about *The Kingdom*. After that, on a number of occasions, he has come to me, sometimes in my sleep and sometimes during my periods of meditation. I look forward to his visits and I have learned things from him that I had no knowledge of before.

"Years ago, when I first encountered you and you told me that you were a shaman, I wondered if you might be the one they were expecting, but I knew that the visit the Beings were awaiting had not yet occurred, so I did not feel at liberty to discuss it with you. Now you have come and from what you have said thus far, I am sure you are the one they were expecting."

"Francis, that is part of what I wanted to talk to you about. They told me about the prophecy that a shaman would come to them from our realm seeking peace. Frankly, I find it a little hard to believe that I am the one they are looking for. I am a shaman, but I am not extraordinary. There are some truly great shamans that I have known. I would expect one of them to be the chosen vessel for such a mission."

"The Spirit quite often works through those of us who are ordinary, Jonathan. It is strange but true. The disciples of Our Lord were really quite ordinary men who were given an extraordinary task. No offense, but you and I are in that category as well. We are not special, but we have a task that is special. I am sure the Spirit could have chosen others who are more capable, but the reality is that the Spirit, for whatever the reasons, has chosen us.

"I'm a rather ordinary monk. I sit next to the abbot at the table because I have been at this monastery longer than anyone else, but I am not a great monk. I was not chosen to be abbot and there are many who are far more knowledgeable and scholarly than I am. But the Spirit has given me the assignment of assisting the shaman chosen to help bring in the new age of *The Kingdom*. My task is to help you understand your mission. I am not worthy of the assignment, but it is mine nonetheless and, unless I choose to disobey the Spirit, I have no choice but to complete my assignment."

"I find all this troubling," said Jonathan as he shifted nervously in his chair. "What you are telling me is giving me further confirmation that I am indeed the one they were awaiting."

"Yes, you are. I am certain of it."

"Francis, I have already met the Being of Light assigned to me for my instruction. But there are some things that are still confusing to both him and to me. Can you please tell me about the coming of *The Kingdom* as understood by Christianity? Why is there no mention of a merger of the two realms?"

"Oh, but there are many references to it, Jonathan. Though most people do not realize it, Christianity is filled with references to the merger. They are hidden from those who do not understand the meaning of the prophecies, but the references are there. It would take time to discuss them all with you, but I am available for that if you wish to stay here longer or can visit often. One of the restrictions placed on us by our order is that we not travel more than five miles from our monastery. It is a strange rule, I know, but it is intended to keep us to our task of seeking the coming of *The Kingdom* where we are, rather than looking for it someplace else."

"I can stay a few days."

"Good. There is much to tell you."

"The silence will be starting again soon. It is part of my discipline. I prefer to observe it, even though at times it is inconvenient. There is another period when conversation is allowed after the evening meal. Perhaps we can continue our discussion at that time."

"I would like that," said Jonathan as he stood to leave. "Thank you for the help you have been to me already."

Francis made a gesture as if to say, "It's nothing," and then added verbally, "I'll see you this evening."

CHAPTER 17

Jonathan used part of the afternoon to take a walk through the monastery and familiarize himself with what was there. He discovered that the entire complex was smaller than he had originally assumed. In addition to the refectory, the wing containing the monks' cells and a rather crude bathroom which he had already seen, there was only a library, a kitchen, some storage rooms and a small chapel.

The library was the largest room of all. It contained a desk for each of the monks and bookshelves holding several thousand books. As Jonathan browsed through the shelves he noted that a great number of the volumes related in some way to the Kingdom of God.

The chapel was simple. Wooden chairs were arranged in a semicircle around a plain wooden table, which served as the altar, and behind it, one clear glass window gave a limited view of the eastern horizon. The four stone walls merged to form a domed ceiling. There were no decorations whatsoever, not even a cross.

The kitchen was unremarkable, modest but more than sufficient for the needs of the small number of inhabitants of the monastery. When Jonathan entered the kitchen, he found James peeling potatoes for the evening meal. He did not look up and did not acknowledge Jonathan's presence in any way.

At first, the stark environment and the lack of verbal

communication were discomforting to Jonathan, but as the afternoon wore on, he found that he was beginning to like it. It started feeling natural to merely nod when encountering another individual in the hallway and he found the environment was conducive to following his own inner process without interruption.

After his exploration of the building, Jonathan spent much of the rest of the afternoon in periods of meditation interspersed with thoughts about what he had learned thus far from Francis and Azar.

The evening meal proceeded as the others, first in silence, then a voiced prayer, followed by the meal itself. After the concluding prayer, when the monks were free to speak again, the abbot approached Jonathan.

"Jonathan, Francis has indicated to me that you will be staying with us a while longer. Please make yourself at home here and join us in any activities or services which you choose to attend. If you have no objection, I will put you in the kitchen for your work assignment. You will be assisting James in the preparation of the meals. You, no doubt, have already experienced some of James' peculiarities, but he can be quite congenial to work with, especially during the periods when we observe silence." The abbot smiled. "At times there are advantages to being a person of few words."

"I would be happy to work with James in the kitchen."

"Good. Let me know if there is any way I can assist you while you are here. Feel free to use the library. I only ask that you not take books back to your cell. It can be quite frustrating to look all through the library for a particular volume that is neatly tucked away under someone's pillow.

"Oh yes, the silence. You are free to speak if it is necessary and there is no way to communicate your needs with a simple gesture. There is no value in going through elaborate gestures and guessing games back and forth to avoid using words. That can be counterproductive. We once had a novice here who, during the silence, tried to communicate through gestures that there was no toilet paper in the bathroom. At first we couldn't figure out what he was doing. The place was in an uproar for weeks over that one.

"Use your common sense. Speak if it is truly necessary. The silence is designed to assist the life of focused contemplation, not to interfere with it.

"Is there any way I can be of help to you now, Jonathan?"

"No. I seem to have everything I need. And thank you for that story about the toilet paper," Jonathan said with a chuckle. "I'll remember that."

The abbot smiled. "Welcome to our midst."

"Thank you."

After the abbot left, Jonathan joined Francis. They returned to his cell.

"There is something I need to explain to you," Francis said after they were seated. "I think it may help you understand the importance of this whole issue of *The Kingdom*.

"Christianity over the years has changed its focus dramatically. In the early years, after the death of Jesus, there was a heavy emphasis on the coming of *The Kingdom*. *The Kingdom* was understood on two levels. On the physical level, *The Kingdom* would bring a new political and social order on earth. On the mystical level, *The Kingdom* would bring a period of miracles and an increased awareness of the realms beyond this one. In the early church the term 'heaven' was used rather loosely to include all levels of existence beyond this one. For *The Kingdom* to 'come on earth as it is in heaven' was understood by many to mean that the veil between the realms would be lifted and there would be a free exchange of information between this realm, the Realm of Light and perhaps some other realms as well.

"Over time, the mystical understanding of *The Kingdom* lost favor and the term came to be understood more in the context of a social order of justice where the will of God would be carried out in earthly affairs.

"I am convinced from my own study, and from what the Beings of Light have told me, that Jesus originally understood *The Kingdom* primarily in terms of a merger of a heavenly realm with our earthly realm. He was definitely concerned about earthly problems, but he believed that the merger of the realms would solve many of them because it would initiate the long-awaited reign of peace and justice in the world and also create a tremendous increase in the frequency of miracles performed by the Beings of Light. His own ministry was a foretaste of what *The Kingdom* would be like. That is why performing miracles was such an important part of his work.

"His Kingdom was 'not of this world.' It drew its power from another realm. When the church started ignoring the reality of other realms, it also lost touch with the essential elements necessary for the coming of *The Kingdom. The Kingdom* will not come without the assistance of the Beings of Light."

"But," interjected Jonathan, "if *The Kingdom* is truly about a merger of the realms, why is that not presented more clearly in the Scriptures? You say that there are many references to it but I don't remember anything that clearly states that a merger of the realms is to occur."

"Jonathan, one of the things that you must understand about prophecy is that it is generally veiled to some degree. It is usually in looking back that one discovers that what was foretold in Scripture has been fulfilled. This same issue came up surrounding the coming of Jesus. There were a great number of prophecies in the scriptures regarding his first coming and the role that he would play. Despite all that, people were utterly surprised by what he was like and the actual form his ministry took when he did come. One of the most common expectations at the time was that the Messiah would be a military ruler, someone who would free his people from political domination by a foreign government. Of course, he did free his people but in a far different way than anyone was expecting. It was only in looking back that people realized the prophecies had indeed been fulfilled.

"The same is true regarding the merger of the realms. There are numerous references to its coming in the words of Jesus himself and elsewhere in the scriptures. What I am suggesting to you is that all of those prophecies about the coming of *The Kingdom* fit with the coming merger of the realms that the Beings of Light have told you and me about. If you look at the scriptures carefully, I think you will see what I mean. And the church, despite having moved away from an understanding of a mystical sort of Kingdom coming on earth, did, in fact, continue to prepare the way for it by making 'we believe in all things visible and invisible' a part of the Nicene Creed. The coming of *The Kingdom* will involve the merger of the visible with what is now invisible to us."

"But, Francis, if you are right about *The Kingdom* involving the merger, why is it that you and I know about it when others don't? Doesn't that destroy that element of surprise about the prophecies?"

"I don't think so, Jonathan. Just as there were some people at the time of Jesus' coming who believed he would not be a military leader, you and I are going counter to common expectations and are looking for the coming of *The Kingdom* in a merger of the realms. There are, however, I'm quite convinced of it, many more surprises in store for us when *The Kingdom* actually comes. I still don't know exactly what *The Kingdom* will be like and neither do the Beings of Light. I suspect that the frequent references to a second coming of Christ are somehow connected to the coming merger of the realms, but I don't know for sure. The

Beings of Light have assured me that the merger will lead to a reign of peace, justice, and miracles, but they have not answered most of my more specific questions about the merger. Most of the details about the merger remain a mystery to me.

"This is an exciting time, Jonathan. I do believe that *The Kingdom* will come very soon, perhaps even during my lifetime. And I believe that you and I have a part to play in its coming."

"Francis, all of this is still a bit overwhelming to me."

"I'm not surprised, Jonathan. It is still a bit overwhelming to me also."

"But, Francis, there is still something that puzzles me. Why did the church let go of its understanding of the existence of other realms?"

"It was largely a political move, Jonathan. Those in power in the church wanted church members to look to them for guidance rather than to beings beyond this realm. They increasingly discouraged contact with other beings and some even proclaimed that such contact was 'of the Devil.' Those who had a mystical understanding of the church and believed in contact with other realms were treated with contempt. The church had become a strong political force and there were many in positions of authority who valued the church's political power more than they valued its spiritual power."

"The church seems so dead now. Francis, the last church service I went to was totally devoid of power."

"Ah! That's part of it, isn't it? The Kingdom has to come for the good of the church as well as for everyone else.

"In the early days, the church was not like that. It was filled with power. There was an expectation that the age of *The Kingdom* was about to begin and there was great excitement surrounding the services because many felt that the services themselves would play a part in ushering in *The Kingdom*. I understand that there was excitement in the Realm of Light as well. Beings of Light regularly attended the services. Usually they were in their invisible form, but not always. They quite often performed miracles and always added a great sense of power to the worship.

"Now, it is quite rare for Beings of Light to show up at a service. Even here at the monastery I rarely sense their presence at the Eucharist. Perhaps they have given up hope. Perhaps they no longer believe that the church will fulfill its purpose of bringing in *The Kingdom*.

"But you and I can help to change all that, Jonathan. We each have access to a Being of Light who is working with us. If we can form such a link, could we not encourage others to form the same kind of link? The Beings encounter people with some regularity in other settings; could we not encourage the Beings to return to our services? A worship service attended by people who sincerely want the Beings to be present might be rather appealing to our friends from the other realm. And if those same people were also asking the Beings to assist them in bringing in *The Kingdom*, it might be extremely appealing."

"I don't know, Francis. That seems too easy. The Beings were disillusioned after putting great hopes in the church before. Why would they believe that the church would be any different now?"

"There is something that might give them a renewed sense of hope."

"What's that?"

"Your coming, Jonathan. You fulfilled their prophecy. You came to them seeking peace. Like most prophecies, its fulfillment came in a different form than they were expecting, but it did come, and that may have given them renewed hope that the age of The Kingdom truly is at hand. I'm not sure, but if they decided to return to our services it just might hasten the coming of *The Kingdom*. I do know that the merger must come forth from both sides, that we must be seeking it at the same time they are seeking it.

"Jonathan, it is almost time for the silence to begin again. We can continue this discussion tomorrow. There is, however, one more thing I would like to share with you tonight.

"I have not discussed this with anyone else here because all the others in the monastery, with the possible exception of James, are rather traditional. They are all seeking *The Kingdom*, but they are not open to any idea as radical as a merger with another realm.

"As you may know, the early church thought that Christ would return and *The Kingdom* would come immediately. The delay in the coming of *The Kingdom* created a crisis of faith in the early church. What occurs to me is that, unlike the Beings of Light, we operate within time. When the merger occurs, perhaps we will be able to experience the absence of time. Perhaps past, present, and future will merge and the coming of Christ and *The Kingdom* will have been just as it was predicted, immediate, quickly, 'in the blink of an eye.'"

"Are you saying that a prophecy about the timing of the coming of *The Kingdom* might be fulfilled when time ceases to exist?"

"Something like that."

"Fascinating! I will have to do some thinking about that."

"Do. It is an issue that intrigues me. I would be quite interested in any thoughts you have about it."

At that point someone walked through the halls ringing a handbell.

"That is the signal that it is time for the silence to resume. I enjoyed our talk. Tomorrow then?"

"Yes."

"Oh yes, Jonathan, I almost forgot. Tomorrow you will be starting your work schedule. Do you also wish to be involved in our worship services? The choice is yours."

Jonathan thought for a moment. "If I find it unbearable

can I leave?"

"Yes, of course."

"OK. I'll give it a try."

"Good. I'll leave a message for Brother James to wake you when he wakes the others.

"Wear something warm, Jonathan. The chapel is quite cold for that first service before sunrise."

"I'll do that. Good night, Francis."

"Good night, Jonathan. I'm glad you are here."

CHAPTER 18

There was a gentle tapping on the door to Jonathan's cell. Instantly he was awake from a sound sleep.

"Yes?" he said, as he stumbled through the dark and opened the door.

"Morning service begins shortly in the chapel," whispered James. "In the future you need only knock back on your door so I know that you are awake. We are still in silence." There was no judgment in James's voice about Jonathan having broken the silence, just a simple statement informing him of their procedures.

"Thank you," whispered Jonathan.

He lit the candle. He could see his breath as he moved around in the small room, a subtle reminder to wear warm clothing for the service. Jonathan dressed quickly and put on his coat, then opened the door, blew out the candle and entered the hall. It was illuminated by one lamp sitting on a small lamp stand halfway down the hall, undoubtedly left there by Brother James so the monks could find their way to the chapel.

There was a sense of quiet about the monastery. Jonathan felt as though he was the only one on the planet as he walked down the empty hall and headed for the chapel.

When he arrived, he saw that most of the monks were already there seated in the small semicircle of chairs facing the bare wooden altar. Jonathan was motioned toward one of the empty seats. Within another minute the remaining two monks entered the chapel and took their seats.

There was a long period of silence. Then the abbot said, "Blessed art thou Lord God of the Universe for separating the night from the day." All present said, "Amen." There was another period of silence, much shorter this time, after which the abbot said, "May we, Lord God, seek the light and may we be illumined within." Again, there was an "Amen." The service proceeded in this fashion for perhaps half an hour. There were various references to light, to its coming into the world and to being transformed by its presence. A period of silence followed each statement. It was simple but quite effective. Jonathan found himself being caught up in the images of light that were presented and longing for a deeper awareness of the Spirit within. The service ended with, "Awaken our souls with the coming of the light and prepare us for service in your Kingdom." Francis started singing a hymn. His voice was clear and beautiful. As the others followed in song, Jonathan was struck by the power of that small group of men singing about the coming of light and life into a world that was waiting in anxious anticipation. Memories of Jonathan's childhood came back. He remembered long-forgotten services he had attended which had generated that same mood of longing for the Spirit's presence. Deep feelings of sadness welled up inside of him. He sensed something tugging at his soul that was deeply moving.

The hymn ended and all filed out of the chapel. The beauty of the hymn was still ringing in Jonathan's ears as they entered the library. Although there was no explanation given, Jonathan realized they were there for one of the regular periods of focused study that the monks engaged in.

After they had taken their seats, Jonathan noticed that there were three empty desks, apparently set aside for visitors. He selected a volume from the shelves entitled *The Coming of the Kingdom* and sat down to read.

The book, as Jonathan soon discovered, was written by a rather wordy scholar without much new to say. But, there was one chapter in the book that intrigued Jonathan. The author was saying that *The Kingdom* was a concept that the church had retained through the centuries despite the delays in its coming and despite rather frequent distortions of its original meaning. He went on to propose that *The Kingdom*, in reality, had less to do with the events of this life than with the cosmological design of the universe and that the reordering of the basic principles on which existence was founded could, among other things, lead to a new order of peace throughout the world. In the new order, previous methods of decision-making and conflict resolution might be totally different.

There it was. In that scholarly book written by a Christian theologian was another suggestion that a radical shift of some sort was to occur before the era of peace on Earth could emerge. Could that shift be the merger of the realms? That would be a shift in the cosmological design of the universe.

The handbell sounded a single time. Some of the monks closed their books immediately; others continued reading briefly and finished up their notes. When all were finished, the group returned in silence to the chapel.

As they entered, Jonathan noticed a small loaf of bread and two small cruets, of wine and of water, sitting on a small table in the back of the chapel.

Through the clear window behind the altar Jonathan could see the faint glow of approaching dawn.

The service began with the ancient words, "Blessed be God: Father, Son, and Holy Spirit," spoken by the abbot, followed by the others responding, "And blessed be his kingdom, now and forever, Amen." Other than more references to light and special prayers for the coming of

The Kingdom, the service proceeded along the same lines as the service Jonathan had attended with Azar. The sermon was about the difficulty of continuing to work for the coming of *The Kingdom* without clear evidence that it was at hand. It ended with a challenge to remain true to one's calling to pray diligently for the coming of *The Kingdom*. The abbot was not an exciting preacher and Jonathan felt a little bored.

As the service progressed, the glow in the eastern sky gradually increased. The sun was rising as the abbot started into the Prayer of Consecration over the bread and wine. As he elevated the bread and cup at the end of the prayer the sun was streaming through the window behind him onto the newly consecrated elements. The abbot paused and said, "Behold, the light of the world." He held the bread and the wine up allowing it to be bathed in the sunlight for perhaps a full minute. All eyes in the room focused on it. Time seemed suspended. Then the abbot abruptly lowered the cup and with a gesture invited all to come forward and receive.

Jonathan was not sure which image was more powerful for him as he came forward. Was he coming to receive life from the sun or from the bread and the wine? The two images were intertwined, but he came forward longing for life, longing for renewal, and longing also for the coming of *The Kingdom*.

The image of the sunlight bathing the bread and wine stayed with him as he left the chapel. It stayed with him as he reported to Brother James in the kitchen; it stayed with him as he scrubbed the kitchen floor on his hands and knees, and it stayed with him when he stirred the pot of hot cereal on the stove. The light and the bread and the wine had merged into a powerful image of new life.

CHAPTER 19

It was after lunch. Jonathan and Francis had returned to Francis' cell to talk.

"How was your morning in the kitchen?" asked Francis.

"It was fine, but I can't say I like scrubbing a stone floor on my hands and knees."

"You'll get used to that," said Francis with a chuckle. "James is a real fanatic about it. He scrubs that floor every morning and every night. It has become a ritual for him. Every person who has ever worked with him in the kitchen complains about it. But at least it doesn't hurt anybody."

"I'm not sure my knees would agree with that," said Jonathan with a wince. Francis smiled.

"James is strange," Francis continued. "There is no doubt about it. But over the years I have grown really fond of him. There is something about him that I really admire. He seems to find meaning in whatever he is doing. He's not good with people but give him a project to do and he brings a sense of life into it. He seems to make things holy simply by his presence. I don't know how else to describe it."

"Well, right now, my knees wish he could find some other way to make the kitchen holy. Now you tell me, why do you have to scrub the floor in the morning if it was scrubbed the night before?"

"Don't ask me! Ask James."

"But I did ask James. He just looked at me. Didn't say a

word, just looked at me. That guy is strange, really strange."

"I'd have to agree with that. He is strange but give it time. There is also something quite special about him. You'll see what I mean.

"But tell me about the rest of your morning, Jonathan. What was your experience of our worship service?"

"Pretty typical in most respects, but that image of the light hitting the newly consecrated bread and wine keeps flashing through my mind. There was something really powerful about that for me."

"I know what you mean. I find it quite meaningful also. I have come to wonder if on some deeper level of the unconscious it speaks to the merger that we have been talking about.

"When I read in the Book of Genesis about God saying 'Let there be light,' I am hit with that same kind of double meaning. Life originally came forth out of the interaction of light with the physical realm and now this new order of *The Kingdom* is to come forth out of the interaction of the Realm of Light with our physical realm. I believe that God is, quite literally, about to bring forth a new creation and that the spark for that creative sequence is, 'Let there be light.'"

"Francis, do you really believe that is what is happening?"

"I am convinced of it. 'Let there be light,' is a command to us. When the Realm of Light merges with our realm, *The Kingdom* will come on earth."

"Do the other monks here believe that?"

"No. At one time or another I have tried to talk to each of them about the importance of the Beings of Light. All of them looked at me a little strange, all of them, that is, except James. When I told him that the Beings of Light had something to do with the coming of *The Kingdom* he said, 'I know.' That's all he said. I could not get him to elaborate on it. But I got a strange feeling that he really did know.

"I have tried to talk to him about the Beings a number of times since then. Each time he just says, "I know," and goes about his business. Once he said, 'I know, but now is not the time...'

"He knows something, Jonathan. I'm not sure what he knows or how he knows it, but he knows something.

"And there is something else. Did you notice what he does during the service?"

"No."

"Watch him tomorrow. He looks at the elevated bread and wine in the sunlight just like the rest of us, but when the celebrant lowers them he kind of squints and glances all around the room like he is looking for something. He's not looking at us; he's looking for something else. Then he goes back to following the service. Watch him tomorrow. You'll see what I'm talking about."

"What do you think he is looking for?"

"I don't know. But I wonder if he could be looking for the Beings of Light. I asked him about it once. He just smiled and went back to work."

"Francis, don't you feel lonely not having anyone to talk to about all this?"

"Yes, sometimes, but I do have Elazar."

"Who is Elazar?"

"He's the Being of Light who comes to me. Talking to him is not quite the same as talking to someone in this realm, but I can speak openly with him."

"What do you talk with him about?"

"Oh, lots of things. Mostly though, he teaches me about his realm and answers a few of my questions about *The Kingdom*. That's his function. He was assigned to teach me. But in the process I have come to know him quite well, in fact, I would have to say that we have become quite good friends. It's rather strange being friends with an angel but that's what we are, friends.

"By the way did you know that they don't really have

wings?"

Jonathan smiled and nodded.

"So, I asked Elazar, 'Then what are those things attached to your back?' And he told me that they don't have anything to do with flying, something about expressions of their energy field. And I said, 'But they look like wings, sort of.' And you know what he said?

"He said, 'I don't care what they look like. They aren't wings. If God had meant for us to have wings he would have created a reason to have them.'"

"I'm not sure I understand."

"I didn't either, Jonathan. So I said, 'What?'"

"And he replied, 'Look. Wings are used to fly through the air, right?' And I answered, 'Right.' So he said, 'And there isn't any air in a nonphysical realm, right?' And I responded, 'Right you are.' And he continued, 'So if God had wanted us to fly with wings, he wouldn't have shown us how to operate in our realm where we move from place to place with our will.' Now that makes sense, doesn't it?"

Jonathan nodded again.

"Then Elazar went on, 'Wings on an angel make about as much sense as wings on a camel. What's a camel going to use wings for? He's already got a way to get around that serves his needs quite well.'"

"Francis, I had a similar discussion with Azar. I always thought that angels had wings too."

"Elazar said, 'Don't believe everything you read in the Bible. Only believe what's true. And it's not true that angels have wings.'"

"Now imagine that, Jonathan! An angel telling you not to believe what's in the Bible! He said that it is as crazy as believing everything you read anywhere else. He said that the people who believe everything they read are fools. I've always thought that myself, but somehow I never thought I would hear an angel tell me that.

"I thought angels would only be concerned with

spiritual stuff. But Elazar isn't. Well I guess it is more accurate to say that he is concerned with spiritual matters, but that's not all he's concerned with. His approach to spirituality is rather practical. He says, 'Believe what's true. And if it's not true but you want it to be true, then believe it and make it true.' And I said to him, 'Then what about angel wings? Can I believe them into reality?' And he said, 'No.' So of course, I said, 'Why not?' And he said, 'Because you couldn't find any self-respecting angel who would be willing to try on a pair of those stupid things!' He really seems to have strong feelings about the whole subject of wings."

"Azar's the same way. But I guess we would get upset if angels kept propagating a myth about us."

"I guess so.

"Well, as I was saying, before I got myself sidetracked on that wings issue, Elazar and I have really become friends. I have grown very fond of him. I don't understand his jokes, but I can put up with that."

"He tells you jokes?"

"Oh yes. He keeps trying to tell me jokes. But most of them are dependent on having some sort of other understanding of reality or they aren't funny. So, I can't understand them. He's tried to explain a few of them to me but I still don't understand them. He says I'm hopeless. And I guess I am when it comes to angel humor. Doesn't Azar try to tell you jokes?"

"Only once."

"Consider yourself lucky. Angel humor is really strange."

"You have gotten me really curious, Francis. Can you give me an example?"

"Well he told me this story about a Being who kept trying to get back to some place he had been before. Elazar thought that was really funny. But I couldn't see anything funny about it. When I asked him to explain it, he said that when any Being tries to get where he has been before, it creates the place not being where it was. I said that I didn't understand. He tried and tried to explain it to me, but I never did understand, and the story never did seem funny to me. Finally, he said, 'Well I guess you just have to understand reality the way angels do in order to appreciate the humor of it.' We left it at that. Or at least I thought we had left it at that. But he doesn't give up. Nearly every time we talk, he makes some sort of comment or tells me some sort of story that strikes him as funny. And I don't get it. Believe me, the only thing that gives me reservations about this merger business is the thought of having to put up with more angel humor.

"Elazar said that angels don't think our jokes are funny either. He said that most of our humor is based on having some sort of surprise ending or a surprise twist in the meaning. He said that since he doesn't operate in the context of time, the beginning, the middle and the end of the joke all occur simultaneously for him. There are no surprise endings. So, jokes of that sort aren't funny to him. But I'm merciful. I don't try to tell him jokes. I wish he would do the same and spare me the agony of listening to his.

"Oh, by the way, Jonathan, back to the wings business. Elazar said that how all that started originally was that someone in our realm asked an angel once what those things attached to his back were and the angel said they were wings. It was angel humor, but the person thought the angel was serious and, since they really do look a lot like wings, the label stuck. Then other angels started telling people in our realm that they had wings. First the angels thought it was funny that we believed they did have wings and then they thought it was funny when most people refused to believe that they didn't have wings. But finally, the whole thing backfired on them and now they feel miffed that the angel wings idea has persisted. You've probably heard that old expression, 'What goes around comes around.' Well, in this case, the angels were laughing at us and now I suspect God is laughing at them."

"If you don't mind my changing the subject ...."

"I would be delighted, Jonathan."

"I was surprised that Azar has a personality and seems to have strengths and weaknesses just like we do. It sounds like you have encountered the same thing in Elazar."

"Yes, I have. I certainly have. It surprised me at first. Frankly, I had always had the impression that angels were perfect, but my experiences with Elazar corrected that misconception in a hurry. He is the most inconsiderate creature I have ever met."

"Really?"

"Yes. And it's not just about him continuing to tell me jokes. He shows up when I'm not expecting him and he never apologizes for it. Much of the time I am delighted to see him, but I can't seem to make him understand that this is not always the case. Once he showed up when I was in the middle of a discussion with the abbot. It was very distracting. The abbot couldn't see him of course, but I could, and Elazar didn't choose to keep quiet either. He kept making comments to me about what the abbot was saying. I really didn't appreciate it and I told him so. I said that he was welcome to come when I was alone but I didn't want him showing up uninvited anymore when I was with someone."

"Did he honor that?"

"No. Two weeks later he did it again. I was furious. What's more, the abbot thought I was furious at him. How do you tell someone that you are angry at an angel who has just shown up unannounced? Has Azar ever done that to you?"

"Once, but I was alone. And as soon as he appeared, he asked if it was all right for him to be there."

"You are indeed a lucky man. If I didn't like Elazar's

other qualities so much I would fire him. I guess you just have to learn to put up with some things you don't like in life."

"Well, Azar is no saint either," Jonathan said with a smile. "He is very self-centered and likes to talk too much. When I first met him, he wouldn't let me get a word in edgewise. He's getting better about it but it's still a problem sometimes."

"I would trade that problem for my problems with Elazar any day.

"Excuse me, Jonathan, but have you heard a bell?

"No."

"Neither have I. I have been enjoying our conversation, but it seems as though we have been talking for quite a long while. Surely it must be past time for the silence to begin. I wonder where James is."

"Maybe he fell asleep or just forgot to ring the bell."

"No, not James. He doesn't take naps and I have never known him to forget anything. He is conscientious to a fault. I am beginning to be concerned. Maybe we had better go check on him."

They went to James' cell and knocked on the door. There was no answer. Francis opened the door and looked in just to make sure. The handbell was sitting on his desk but there was no sign of James.

They checked the library and the chapel, but there was no sign of him there either. They broke the silence and asked the other monks they encountered if any of them had seen James. None had.

"Francis, we haven't checked the kitchen yet. Maybe he's there."

"Maybe," said Francis as they hurried in that direction, "but the cleanup after lunch was almost finished when we left for my cell. I have never known James to start on supper preparation until midafternoon. What time did he tell you to be there?"

"He said that it was going to be a simple meal tonight and that I didn't need to be there until an hour before dinner."

"Something's wrong. I know it!" said Francis as they rushed through the refectory on the way to the kitchen.

James was lying unconscious on the kitchen floor amid some broken dishes. There was a jagged gash just above his right temple. Blood was still oozing from it, forming a dark red pool on the stone floor.

"He must have slipped on the wet floor. Go get the abbot. Quick!"

Francis knelt beside James as Jonathan rushed out to find the abbot.

Jonathan found him overseeing some repairs to a rock wall a short distance from the building. By the time Jonathan returned with him, all the other monks in the building had heard the commotion and had crowded around the door to the kitchen. The abbot pushed his way through.

The abbot had some medical training prior to his call to the monastery. He examined James' head carefully, checked his pulse and breathing and lifted each eyelid.

"I don't know a lot about medicine," the abbot said finally, "but I do know enough to tell you that this is serious. He appears to have slipped on the floor and must have hit his head on the edge of the table. There is another wound that is not bleeding that was probably caused when his head hit the stone floor. I'm really more concerned about the second wound. His pulse is weak, and his pupils are not the same size. That can indicate brain damage.

"Matthew," he said to the youngest man in the group, "take the South Trail down to the village. It's steep but if you hurry you can make it down that way in five or six hours. Find a doctor that can come back with you; I know that won't be easy; and get back as quick as you can." The monk left. "The earliest we can hope to have a doctor here is sometime tomorrow," he said to the group. "We have got to do the best we can until then."

The abbot carefully bandaged James' head, then supervised the construction of a stretcher out of some poles and a blanket, and had James moved back to his cell. A prayer vigil for James' recovery was instituted in the chapel and Francis volunteered to take the first shift sitting with James in his cell.

The abbot approached Jonathan privately. "Rumor has it that you are a shaman," he said. "I am a very traditional man. I only know one path and I follow it. I'm not really sure what you do or how you do it, but if you have any healing powers you can bring to bear you are more than welcome to try. I am open to anything that might help James. Without some sort of miracle, I don't think he will survive."

"There are different types of shamans," replied Jonathan. "I function as an adviser and as a contact with other realms of reality. I am not really a healer, but I will do what I can. I too will be praying for James and am ready to assist in any way I can."

"Would you be willing to spell Francis as a sitter with James?"

"Yes, I would be honored to do that."

"Thank you, Jonathan."

The abbot placed a hand on Jonathan's shoulder and then turned and left the room. Jonathan was left with a feeling of awe. He was merely a visitor at the monastery, and yet he was being fully included in the life of that community, not only in their worship services, but even in their most intimate of all struggles, the struggle with death itself.

CHAPTER 20

"We beseech thee to send thy holy angels to watch over thy servant James and to minister him in his hour of need."

"WE BESEECH THEE TO HEAR US GOOD LORD."

"We beseech thee to ease his suffering and to restore him to wholeness of body, mind and spirit."

"WE BESEECH THEE TO HEAR US GOOD LORD."

"We beseech thee to give him power over the enemy and to restore him to wholeness of life."

"WE BESEECH THEE TO HEAR US GOOD LORD."

It was well after midnight. The abbot was leading the community in the traditional Litany for Healing that had been used in his order for hundreds of years. The abbot had led the Litany every hour since the vigil had started that afternoon. All agreed that all work would be suspended and that prayer for James would be the primary focus of the community until he improved, or, although no one said it, until he died. The monks were free to come and go from the chapel as they chose, but most had remained there praying for James almost continuously since the vigil began.

Jonathan and Francis had exchanged places caring for James every two hours. The abbot had come by repeatedly to check on James' condition and to take vital signs throughout the day. James had continued to deteriorate. His breathing grew more shallow and irregular. All signs indicated that death was drawing near.

Jonathan was sitting quietly with James listening to the labored breathing and praying for him. Suddenly Jonathan became aware of another presence in the room. He looked up and saw Azar standing beside the bed.

"He doesn't look so good, does he?" said Azar.

"Azar, I'm glad you are here. I was hoping you might come."

"Are you sure? I don't want to intrude."

"No. I'm very glad to see you."

"Rumor has it in our realm that special prayers are being said at this monastery, including some that are asking for the presence of angels. When those responsible for making our assignments heard that you were here, they decided to send me to check it out. As you know, we don't show up automatically merely because someone mumbles a request for angels in some liturgy or other. The people making those requests usually don't have any real desire or expectation that we will actually come. What makes it different in this case is that you and Francis and James are all here in the same place at the same time. Since all three of you have significant links to our realm it gives the request for our presence a bit more credibility. So here I am.

"Do you really want some of us to come, Jonathan?"

"Absolutely, Azar. I do and I'm sure that Francis wants that too. And we have reason to suspect that James would have wanted a visitation of Beings of Light also. But obviously we can't ask him now. In fact, it is the need for James' healing that has led to using the liturgy requesting the presence of angels in the first place. I can't actually speak for the others, but I do know that everyone in the community is quite concerned about James and truly wants him to recover."

"Jonathan, my instructions are to see if the community at large is ready to take on the responsibility that a visitation from us would engender. James is visiting our realm at this present moment of your time. He has indicated to us that he is not anxious to return to your realm unless it is really important. He has gotten a sense of what the afterlife is like and would rather go on in that existence than return to yours. But, he is willing to return if, and only if, his presence in your world would truly make a difference in carrying out the plan."

"What plan?"

"The Plan. The Spirit's plan for the merger of the realms."

"Oh."

"Our concern is about the abbot. He has a very rational approach and is not generally open to spiritual encounters beyond his normal range of experience. If we assist in bringing about the healing of James we are concerned that the abbot will simply consider it an amazing medical recovery and will continue to ignore the need for continued interaction between our two realms. The abbot's rational approach could block the unfolding of the Spirit's plan for this monastery. James is not willing to return unless the coming of *The Kingdom* is ready to proceed. There you have it."

"So, Azar, you are asking me if the abbot is open to an encounter between the realms. Is that right?"

"That is correct."

"I don't know. I don't really know him very well. He has been nice to me and he even invited me to function as a healer if it would help James."

"Well at least that's encouraging. What did you say?"

"Basically, I said that although some shamans are healers, I am not. That my usual function is to work as an adviser to people and as an intermediary for the flow of information between realms."

"Perfect! What did he say to that?"

"Well basically, he had indicated that a miracle was needed to save James and asked me to do anything I could."

"I see. Don't go away, Jonathan. I'll be right back."

Azar faded from view and returned almost instantly.

"There is a great deal of excitement over here," said Azar. "The teachers are of the opinion that this monastery may in fact be the bridgehead, so to speak, where the merger is to first occur. Your presence, Francis' presence and James' presence and injury at this particular point in your time all seem to be fitting together as though they are part of the Spirit's plan. You have got to understand, Jonathan, that the three of you are no ordinary triad of beings.

"One of our Beings has been going to Francis and working with him for quite some time. His assignment was to help Francis understand the true nature of *The Kingdom* and the importance of the merger.

"James has been coming to us for just as long. He found his way here, as you did, and fell in love with our realm. He asked if he could return and learn more about us. He is rather peculiar, as you may have noticed, and at first that caused the teachers to have some uncertainty about how much to share with him, but we found him to be absolutely sincere and trustworthy. He is amazingly perceptive, and he has kept everything that he has learned absolutely confidential. That was one of the conditions set up by the teachers, that he not share what he has learned with anyone until the merger is under way. Because he is so strange, there was some concern that if he talked openly about what he was learning he might be shipped out for psychiatric treatment. Although James doesn't function so well with people in your realm, he is amazingly agile and perceptive when he is in our realm. He has proved to be a truly unusual find for us and there is no one in your realm who understands us a thoroughly as James does.

"We thought it might be significant that both Francis and James were from the same little obscure monastery that was dedicated to praying for the coming of *The Kingdom*.

But when you, the fulfillment of our prophecy, showed up there also, let me tell you, all the teachers took notice. Something is about to happen here. I am convinced of it. Most of the teachers are convinced of it too. And the number of volunteers that are lining up over here to attend services at the monastery is amazing, absolutely amazing. Until you showed up there was hardly anyone who was willing to attend, monastery or not.

"This could well be the point in your time, and the place, where the merger could occur. But this whole thing is really quite fragile and could fail if the abbot is not responsive. He is the weak link.

"We have discussed all this in our realm at great length. This is what we suggest; that you go to the abbot and tell him that the healing of James is indeed possible but that it all depends on him. You should explain that you have made contact with our realm and that we are issuing him a special invitation to visit our realm tonight. Stress that the offer is good only for a short time. He must come tonight. By tomorrow night it will be too late.

"If he comes, we will explain about the merger and see if we can enlist his aid. If he doesn't come, then nature will take its course and James will die physically sometime tomorrow.

"Conditions are ripe for the merger now. If this opportunity is missed it may be many years of your time before an opportunity will come again. Are you willing to give it a try?"

"Absolutely!"

"All right, Jonathan, I will get a message to Elazar who, in turn, will tell Francis to come spell you now. James is getting weaker. We don't have much time!" Azar paused. "It just struck me what I said. 'We don't have much time.' I'm feeling it, Jonathan! For the first time, I'm feeling the pressure of time! This is weird." He looked intently at Jonathan. "Pray for success, Jonathan. Pray hard for success!" Then he disappeared.

CHAPTER 21

A few minutes later, Francis quietly opened the door to James' cell and came in.

"How is he doing?" Francis spoke in a whisper.

"I think he is a little weaker."

Francis frowned as he looked at James' labored breathing.

"Elazar showed up again. Right in the middle of the Litany for Healing. Didn't apologize for the interruption, just showed up. He said that a lot was going on and that I needed to spell you right away. That's all he said. So I came. What's this all about?"

"There's no time to explain everything right now. I'll give you all the details as soon as I can. There is a possibility that the merger might start here at this monastery. I have to go talk to the abbot right away."

"Are you going to tell him about the merger?" asked Francis as he exchanged places with Jonathan in the tiny room.

"Not me. The Beings of Light plan to do that."

"That should be interesting," said Francis as he rolled his eyes. "I'll pray for them and for him."

"Do that," said Jonathan as he was closing the door. "And throw one in for me too; if you don't mind."

Jonathan made his way to the chapel. The abbot was just finishing the Litany when Jonathan entered. Jonathan went over to him and whispered that he needed to talk to him. The abbot got up and followed Jonathan out of the chapel and back to the refectory.

"Is it about James?" asked the abbot. He looked concerned.

"Indirectly. I had a visitation from one of the Beings of Light."

"The what?"

"Beings of Light. You might call them angels."

"You're putting me on," said the Abbot with a chuckle.

"No. I'm absolutely serious.

"Look, you said earlier that I was welcome to try to heal James. I'm not a healer, but I can make contact with other realms. I can't heal James but the Beings of Light can. One of them made contact with me tonight and said that they could heal James only if James were free, after his recovery, to fulfill a certain mission he has. It all depends on you."

"What do you mean?"

"You are the abbot. You can give him permission to teach the others here, and any visitors that come, about what he knows about the Beings of Light."

"Is this some kind of joke?"

"No."

"You're asking me to give James permission to give classes about angels?"

"Yes."

He looked intently at Jonathan. "You are serious, aren't you?"

"Yes, I am."

"I don't even believe in angels."

"That's what we figured. So, we have arranged for you to meet some."

"To meet some angels?"

"Yes. They want to show you their realm and tell you

about something that is very important. I realize that this may seem very strange to you right now, but all of this is far more important than you know. And James' recovery depends on it."

The abbot looked at Jonathan. He was obviously trying to make sense of it all. Finally, he said, "Can I think about this?"

"I'm afraid not. There isn't much time. James is getting weaker. Without a miracle he will be dead in a few hours. I'm afraid you'll just have to trust me on this one."

The abbot stared a Jonathan again. Then he said slowly, "I want you to know that I still think this is crazy. I don't believe in angels and I think anybody who claims to have seen one needs to have their head examined. But I care a lot about James and if there is even the slightest chance that this is a way to help him, I'm willing to give it a try. What do I have to do?"

Jonathan breathed a sigh of relief. "You don't have to do anything except sit here and meditate. One of the Beings will come to you."

"If this does work, Jonathan. You notice, I said *if.* If this does work, I'm not going to die or anything, am I?"

"No, you're not going to die. Your life may change dramatically, but you won't die."

"OK. I just sit here and meditate?"

"That's right. They'll take care of the rest."

The abbot closed his eyes.

Jonathan closed his eyes.

They waited for perhaps five interminable minutes. Then Azar spoke.

"I'm here," he said.

Jonathan opened his eyes. There was Azar standing before them as luminous as ever.

"You can open your eyes now," Jonathan said to the abbot.

The abbot opened his eyes and gasped, "Holy Mother

of God!"

"This is Azar," said Jonathan.

The abbot blinked. "I don't believe my eyes."

"That's all right," said Jonathan. "I realize that this is quite a shock.

"Azar, I guess you don't need me anymore right now, do you?"

"No. Thank you for your help though. I'll let you know how things go."

Jonathan stood up and started walking out of the room.

Azar began, "Now, Abbot, I hope you don't mind me calling you that. There are a lot of things I need to tell you and show you and there are some other Beings of Light that you need to meet. You aren't scared are you? There is nothing to be scared of really, but I have been told that beings from your realm are often scared when they have their first encounter with one of us. This is your first encounter with a Being of Light, isn't it? I think that is so interesting. "Why I remember when I first met Jonathan. He just showed up in our realm and said he wanted to learn about peace. Now that's a long story, but you don't have time for all of that now, do you? I guess we'll have to skip that. Are you ready? Now first, there are a few things I need to explain to you so you will understand what this is all about. Do you have any questions right now? Well of course you do. All of this is new to you, isn't it? Well just relax and we will explain it all. You see there is this matter of the Kingdom...."

Jonathan shook his head and laughed to himself as he headed down the hallway toward James' cell. "I don't know which is going to be the bigger challenge for the abbot. Helping to bring in *The Kingdom* or getting a word in in the midst of Azar's monologue. Azar's really wound up tonight."

CHAPTER 22

Jonathan gently opened the door to James' cell and looked in. Francis looked up and motioned for Jonathan to enter.

"What happened?" asked Francis. "I expected you to be engaged a good deal longer than that."

"Well, basically, I told the abbot that the Beings of Light wanted to meet him and show him their realm."

"Did he believe you?"

"No, he didn't. But he agreed to attempt a meeting anyway. We meditated, Azar showed up, and the last thing I saw when I left was Azar talking a blue streak while the abbot just sat there with his mouth open like he had just seen a ghost. It was really rather amusing."

Francis laughed. "I would love to have seen that." Then he looked more serious. "I'm very concerned about James. He is getting worse."

Jonathan looked at James. His breathing was shallow and even more labored. "I see what you mean. Well, there is nothing we can do now except wait and pray. Within a couple of hours, we should know the outcome with regard to the abbot. Everything rests on that."

Jonathan stayed with James while Francis returned to the chapel and, at the appointed time, led the Liturgy for Healing in the abbot's absence. The hours passed slowly.

Finally, there was a gentle tap on the door to the cell. Jonathan opened it expecting to see Francis.

It was the abbot.

"I came by to check on James. I don't have time to talk now. It's time to begin the morning Eucharist."

The abbot quickly checked James pulse and breathing. Jonathan looked for any clue in the abbot's manner that would reveal how the abbot had responded to his encounter with the Beings of Light.

"What..." started Jonathan. But the abbot held up a hand.

"I must start the service. We'll talk later."

The abbot squeezed past Jonathan and walked quickly down the hall.

Shortly afterward, Francis arrived to spell Jonathan.

"Francis, the abbot was here to check on James. He left not two minutes ago."

"What did he say?"

"Nothing. Just that he had to rush because it was time for the service to start and that we would talk later."

"Well how did he seem? Could you tell whether things went well or not?"

"Francis, I haven't a clue. He was in and out of here like a flash."

"The suspense is killing me, Jonathan, but I guess there is nothing we can do except wait.

"I'm here to relieve you. See you in a couple of hours."

Jonathan left the cell and went to the chapel. He arrived just as the service was starting.

"Blessed be God, Father, Son, and Holy Spirit." said the abbot.

"AND BLESSED BE HIS KINGDOM NOW AND FOREVER. AMEN," responded the monks.

The service proceeded as usual. The sermon stressed the importance of keeping one's faith and of continuing to pray for the coming of *The Kingdom*.

There was no clue, no hint, in the abbot's words or mannerisms that anything unusual had transpired that night. Right before the Offertory the abbot told the congregation that he had visited James right before the service and that he was still "gravely ill." He asked that they all continue to keep James in their prayers.

The service proceeded with the consecration of the bread and the wine. As before, the abbot lifted the newly consecrated bread and wine up into the shaft of sunlight.

And then it happened.

The chapel was filled with light, sunlight and light from another source. There were Beings of Light everywhere, fifteen, twenty, maybe more. The room pulsed with energy. And Azar was there standing with the rest of them right behind the abbot as the bread and the chalice were lowered.

The monks seemed to sense that something had happened. Some of them looked around the room. Jonathan couldn't tell whether they could see the Beings or not, but they were obviously being affected by something.

The abbot smiled as he proceeded with the service. The bread and wine were distributed. The Post Communion Prayer was said. The Blessing and Dismissal were given. Immediately the monks started mumbling and talking among themselves. They seemed excited. Jonathan pushed past them and left the chapel. He ran down the hall to James's cell. He paused for a moment trying to catch his breath and then knocked.

Francis opened the door.

"How is James?" Jonathan asked, breathing hard.

"Well I'm not sure. His breathing pattern shifted a couple of minutes ago. I'm not certain but I think he is sleeping now."

Jonathan checked. The change was dramatic. James was breathing comfortably, a man in a deep and peaceful sleep. The Beings had obviously been here as well.

"Elazar came," said Francis. "There were two other Beings with him. They came. They lingered a minute or two without saying anything and then left. It's happening, isn't it? They showed up at the service too, didn't they?"

Jonathan nodded. "Lots of them. And they brought the power with them. The monks are buzzing with excitement.

"Francis, I could shoot the abbot! He played it all the way through with a poker face, mediocre sermon, the works. He didn't give a clue that anything was different right up to the elevation of the bread and wine. Then it happened. The room filled with light and there they were, Beings were everywhere.

"The abbot just smiled and continued with the service. But I can tell you, it was like no service I have ever attended before. There was power there. It was alive."

"Do you think *The Kingdom* is really coming now?"

"I wouldn't be surprised."

At that moment the abbot arrived.

"How is James?" he asked.

"Come in and see for yourself," said Jonathan, as he and Francis stepped into the hallway to make room.

The abbot examined James and then joined them in the hall.

"Just as I thought," said the abbot, "sleeping when he should have been in chapel."

They all laughed. James, partly roused by the noise, rolled over and started snoring loudly.

"I don't guess we have to worry about him anymore," said Francis.

"Now," said the abbot, "all I have to worry about is the kind of reputation we are going to get when he starts opening his mouth and teaching about those fool Beings of Light.

"Jonathan, is Azar the one who regularly gets together with you?"

"Yes," said Jonathan.

"My sympathies! He's more neurotic than any person I know. Talked constantly. I couldn't say a thing. He'd ask me questions and then go right on talking without giving me a chance to answer."

"He's like that sometimes," said Jonathan, "but I've grown rather fond of him. He means well. He's just a little self-absorbed at times."

"If last night is any indicator, I would say that he's extremely self-absorbed."

"He's been working on it," replied Jonathan, "and he has gotten a lot better. He was probably just nervous, meeting you for the first time and all. And I doubt if it helped that you don't believe that angels even exist."

"Well, I didn't but I sure do now. I can tell you, it was a shock to see Azar standing there right in front of me. But that shock was small in comparison to the shock of discovering that they aren't perfect. I still can't get over how self-centered that Azar was. Well, enough of that.

"There's a lot of work to be done. *The Kingdom* is at hand and despite all our talk about it through the years, we really aren't ready for it."

The abbot started to leave the cell.

"Wait," said Francis. "Aren't you going to tell us what happened last night?"

"No."

"No?" said Jonathan and Francis together.

"Well actually, no, not now. I have too much to do. But I have decided to call a meeting of the community this morning after breakfast and I will tell all of you then, in detail, what happened. It was the strangest but most glorious night of my life."

The abbot pushed past them and walked down the hallway whistling a hymn to himself.

"Now that's strange." said Francis. "I've never seen him so happy."

"Whatever happened when he was with the Beings of Light must have been really good," added Jonathan.

CHAPTER 23

The meeting scheduled for that morning was postponed and then postponed again. The abbot said that he did not want to have the meeting without James present and James slept most of the day. The sense of excitement among the monks continued to build throughout the day. Several of the monks reported seeing luminous Beings in the building. Others saw nothing but reported sensing some sort of "Holy Presence."

Jonathan slept after lunch until he was awakened to assist with the preparation of the evening meal.

Late in the afternoon James woke up on his own and was first seen when he walked into the kitchen.

"What's going on here?" he asked as he came through the door and saw that Jonathan was well along in the preparation of the evening meal. "I must have fallen asleep. Why didn't someone wake me?"

News that James was awake spread quickly and everyone, including the abbot, was soon crowded into the kitchen to hear what he had to say. The abbot announced that the rule of silence was not in effect until further notice. James seemed confused by all the excitement and the questions about how he was feeling. He said that he had had a "beautiful dream" but had no memory of the fall or anything else over the past 24 hours. He was not even aware that his head was bandaged until his attention was called to it. When the bandage was removed, there was not even a hint of a scar at the site where the gash had been. The abbot explained to him that he had almost died from a fall and that the whole community had been praying for him. James thanked the community for their prayers and then said, "Look, I'm really not enjoying all this attention. If you want anything to eat tonight you had better clear out of here and let Jonathan and me get our work done." He picked up a wooden spoon and playfully brandished it as he shoved the others, including the abbot, out of the kitchen.

James talked amicably to Jonathan as they finished the meal preparations. The aloofness that had been so characteristic of James in the past was gone.

At one point, Azar and another Being of Light, whom Jonathan later learned was Elazar, glided into the kitchen and in comic fashion pretended to taste the soup. James looked shocked at first and then smiled and said nothing.

"By the way," said Jonathan, "I think it's all right to talk about the Beings now. Various ones have been hanging around the monastery ever since they showed up at the Eucharist this morning. The abbot had an encounter with them last night. He is going to tell us all about it at a meeting after dinner."

"That should be interesting," said James. "I never thought the abbot would be open to anything beyond the realm of logic and systematic theology."

"A lot seems to be changing around here," replied Jonathan.

"Obviously," said James. "I even feel different." Then he turned to Azar and Elazar who were still playing around the pot of soup. "Out of here!" he shouted playfully at them. "Just because you heal somebody doesn't mean you are invited to dinner." The Beings glided out of the kitchen.

Jonathan laughed.

"Apparently you realize that it was the Beings of Light

that healed you."

"Yes. That's one of their functions."

"What can you tell me about *The Kingdom*?" asked Jonathan.

"Only what they have told me. Actually, that's quite a lot. But perhaps we should wait until the abbot's meeting before we get into all that. The Beings told me not to talk about it openly until the abbot publicly announced his belief in the reality of angels. For a while, I thought that was their way of saying that I was never to speak openly about them. But it sounds like the abbot has something to tell us tonight. We'll see."

CHAPTER 24

Everyone was in a good mood at supper that evening. The abbot had continued the suspension of the silence and the meal was filled with conversation and jokes. James was as outgoing as anyone present.

After the dishes were cleared the abbot asked everyone to have a seat in the refectory because there were "some things I want to tell you."

Jonathan looked around the room. Not only were all the monks present, but the room was also crowded with Beings of Light.

The abbot spoke. "Let me start off by saying that I believe in angels." Jonathan looked at James. There was a wide grin on his face. "Twenty-four hours ago, I would have told you that they were purely mythological or some sort of religious hallucination. But when your experience outstrips your beliefs you have to make an adjustment in your beliefs. I had an experience last night that caused me to make that shift. Not only did I meet an angel, or Being of Light, if you prefer, but I was transported to their realm of existence and experienced things that defy description. Some of you have seen Beings of Light for the first time today. Others have not seen them but have told me that they have sensed a 'Holy Presence' in our midst. However, you may have experienced them, let me assure you that what you have experienced is quite real.

"As you know, Jonathan came to visit us a few days ago. He came seeking peace and an understanding of *The Kingdom.*

"Now this is where it starts to get really interesting. Jonathan had apparently contacted the Beings of Light at some point and had been told by them that a partial merger of their realm with our realm was about to take place and that the merger was an essential element in the coming of *The Kingdom.* Last night the Beings of Light showed me that there are a number of veiled references to such a merger in our Scriptures. Once you look at those verses from the perspective of a coming merger they do all seem to fit together and describe an interaction of the realms that is quite intense and different from anything previously experienced. But I am getting ahead of myself.

"Last night Jonathan introduced me to an angel named Azar. His body was made entirely of light and he even had wings, or what appeared to be wings. Azar adamantly insisted that they are not wings, so I guess I don't know what they are. But anyway, Azar started telling me about the coming of *The Kingdom* and about the coming merger of two realms, our physical realm and Azar's, which he called the Realm of Light. He took me to his realm and showed me what it is like. I wish I could adequately describe it to you. It was beautiful beyond words and yet everything, including Azar, was constructed entirely of light. I even saw a beautiful city made of light, like the one described in the Book of Revelation.

"I met with a group of Beings who, I was told, serve as teachers in their realm. I suppose 'theologians' is really a more accurate term for their role. They are the ones who showed me various veiled references in our own Scriptures to a coming merger. They also told me that they are of the opinion that this monastery is to play a unique role in the breaking forth of *The Kingdom* on earth. They believe it is here, in this monastery, that the merger will begin. I find that quite exciting, to say the least.

"They said that they are now willing to return to the Eucharist in large numbers and that our services will once again be filled with power, as they were in the early days of Christianity. Healings and other manifestations of power will be quite common again and the Beings will make their presence known in a variety of ways. Some individuals will be able to see them with no difficulty.

"Now some of that has already started to occur here. This morning I saw a number of Beings present at our service. I believe some of you did too. And James was healed. The interaction between the two realms is increasing dramatically. Or to put it another way, *The Kingdom* is starting to come here on earth as it is in Heaven.

"Incidentally, I was told by the Beings that the term Heaven had a much broader context in the early Church. Many understood it to mean any realm of existence beyond our own.

"The Beings explained that it is the coming together of the Realm of Light and our own physical realm that constitutes *The Kingdom of Heaven on Earth*. And it is starting to happen here, now, in this place.

"But the coming of *The Kingdom* is not just for our benefit. The Beings of Light have told me that they need to be able to experience time and some of the limitations of physical existence in order to enhance their own development. Strange as it may seem to us, many of the Beings of Light have been longing for the ability to experience reality in the more limited way that we do. The rate of their spiritual development is hampered at times by their lack of limitations. Our realm, it appears, is ideally suited to dealing with emotional issues and psychological conflict. The Beings of Light assure me that the conditions that we have are really quite unique and they wish to take advantage of them. And they want the opportunity to learn from us about some of the dynamics of interpersonal relationships. They are anxious to establish personal relationships with us and to experience the limitations of time and space that we humans struggle with.

"I hope this is not the case, but I am aware that what I have been saying this evening may seem to be the wild ravings of a psychotic fool. All I can say is that what I experienced was quite real and I truly believe that what we have been praying for for so many years, the coming of *The Kingdom*, is now finally starting to unfold in a way far different from what any of us ever imagined when we joined this order. We dedicated ourselves to working and praying for the coming of *The Kingdom*. For years we experienced the frustration and disappointment of waiting and working and praying for the coming of *The Kingdom* without seeing any results. Many of you have complained in your private conversations with me that our worship services seem flat and meaningless. I have shared your struggle. At times it was only our faith in Christ's teachings about *The Kingdom* that kept us on our task.

"A new day dawned this morning. A day filled with power and excitement: a day filled with the presence of the holy angels in our midst. Were there any of you who found this morning's Eucharist flat and meaningless?" The group laughed. "I guess not. I can tell you that, for me, the service was one of the most meaningful experiences of my entire life. Our Church, which has seemed so empty and incomplete for so long, is now filled with power and possibility. It is not what we did that caused all of this to happen. It is the coming of the Beings of Light to our service that has changed it for me, changed it for us.

"To those Beings of Light who are here with us in this meeting tonight... For any of us mortals who are not able to see them, they are standing all around the edges of this room. To you Beings of Light, I wish to express our most sincere gratitude for what you have given us by your presence with us at this morning's service and throughout the day. And I particularly wish to thank you for restoring James to health. In the hours after his injury, when it looked as though he would surely die, I felt a great sense of personal loss. He has become dearer to me than a brother, no pun intended.

"And James, to you, I wish to say welcome back. We have missed you. We are glad you chose to return to us." There was a chorus of Amens from the monks that sounded like a congregation at a Baptist revival. The monk who was sitting next to James gave him a hug. Others turned around in their seats and gave him a pat on whatever part of him they could reach.

"And Azar, I have a few words for my special guide to the Realm of Light. Thank you." Jonathan turned and looked at Azar. He was pulsing with pride. "Thank you for showing me your realm. Thank you for giving me all the information that you shared with me. I listened to profound truths coming forth from you." The abbot smiled. "I listened, and I listened, and I listened. I had to listen. I couldn't get a word in edgewise!" Azar smiled sheepishly. The room laughed, but the angels, including Azar, laughed the hardest of all. When the room grew quiet again, the abbot continued. "And thank you for your laughter, Azar, and for being a good sport. The laughter of angels is the most beautiful sound I have ever heard."

The abbot looked around the room again at all the Beings of Light. "You have given us a wonderful gift. You have given us your presence. You have given us your laughter. You have given us your power. Words cannot express how deeply grateful I am to all of you."

Then to Jonathan and the assembled monks the abbot said, "Gentlemen, *The Kingdom* has come. It broke forth upon us here this morning during our service. It is breaking forth upon us even now as we speak and celebrate and laugh together. I have never felt so whole. And I suspect that our Church has never been so whole. We have prayed for years for the coming of *The Kingdom* and now it is truly here. It is time now for us to join efforts with the Beings of Light and establish *The Reign of Peace* throughout the world. Unless we share the message, or rather, share the experience, *The Kingdom* will not come to all people. The Apostles were called to spread the message of the Gospel throughout the world. We are called to go forth now and spread the message that *The Kingdom* has not just drawn near, it has arrived. The Church that has been incomplete through the centuries is now ready to move into an era of wholeness. As we join with the Beings of Light, we, as a Church, we, as a people, become whole.

"I don't know what the future holds for us here or for the Church. We have gotten but the first glimpse of *The Kingdom* here today. *The Kingdom* must unfold. As it unfolds, we will undoubtedly be led into experiences beyond our wildest dreams.

"When the angels appeared to the shepherds and announced the birth of Jesus, they also brought a message of hope for peace and goodwill on earth. Thus far we have not been able to establish lasting peace in the world or in ourselves. Now we have a chance. The Beings of Light are willing to show us the path to peace. They tell me that the first step in the process is the merger of the realms. Somehow I know that they are correct. I can't quite explain it, but my contact with Azar and the other Beings is bringing about a change in me. Already I am starting to feel more whole and more at peace. We have all been told that simply finding God will give us inner peace. But that peace is delivered by the Beings of Light. Bringing peace is their special gift to us. It is when we knowingly, or unknowingly, encounter the Beings of Light and experience God working through them that we begin to taste true peace. That is 'the peace which passes all understanding.' It comes through an encounter with the realm beyond our own.

"We monks have been waiting here, cloistered, for years,

waiting here for the coming of *The Kingdom*. Now *The Kingdom* has come and it is time for our order to go forth and share the news. We must help *The Kingdom* come to the rest of the world as well. But let us not forget that the coming of *The Kingdom* is but the first step. Living in *The Kingdom*, living in the relationship that we have established here between the realms, is what *The Kingdom* is all about. *The Kingdom* has come on earth. We are being made whole. The reign of peace has begun.

"I have been rambling long enough."

The abbot sat down. The room was quiet.

Jonathan felt profoundly moved and humbled by the importance of the role he and Azar had played in opening the way for the merger that was now taking place, but he knew that his mission was not yet complete. The realms had merged in this one isolated place in a monastery that few even knew existed. Clearly the news of what had happened here needed to be shared, but what after that? The next steps on the path to peace remained unknown to him.

James rose and addressed the group. "We have started something new here today. We have merged our energy and our enthusiasm and our resources. But all of us have not yet merged our minds. The Beings taught me many things over the last years that I was not allowed to share with anyone. Now, at last, I have their permission to speak openly and to share what I have learned with any and all who wish to learn. The search for peace caused Jonathan to journey to the Realm of Light. There was a prophecy that a shaman would come to that realm from ours seeking peace. That occurred when Jonathan visited their realm.

"There are prophecies in the Bible about the coming of *The Kingdom* and *The Reign of Peace on Earth*. The merger of the realms has begun, *The Kingdom* is finally at hand, but I believe that our work will always be unfinished if we do not press on to the issue of establishing true and lasting peace among nations. All efforts along those lines in the past have failed. Is the establishment of bonds of friendship and cooperation between the realms enough to bring world peace? I wish that it were that simple, but I strongly suspect that it is not.

"The Beings have told me that the merger is an essential part of the process, but that there are other things that must be done after the merger occurs. The Beings themselves do not know all of the steps in the process, but they tell me that our inability to take advantage of our limitations hampers the process. I am not sure what they mean by that, but I suspect that the desire most of us have to be free of limitations blinds us to the importance of accepting our limitations as a gift from God. The angels tell me that both personal and spiritual growth are greatly enhanced by embracing one's limitations. As I said, I am not sure what they mean by that, but they assure me that they long for the opportunity to function in a realm with limitations because their growth is hampered by their lack of the limitations imposed by time and space. It does occur to me that many of our conflicts with other people revolve around not wanting to accept limitations. Our quest for power stems from our fantasy that we will be happy if we have unlimited money and possessions. It is ironic that we long for a lack of limitations while the angels long for limitations. Perhaps when we learn to live in harmony with the angels we will be able to live in harmony with our fellow human beings as well.

"Peace exists in the Realm of Light but we have not been able to achieve lasting peace on earth. Why is that? The angels have told me that it is possible for peace and disagreement to coexist in our realm. In the past we have tried to achieve lasting peace through reaching agreements between individuals and nations, but we have never been successful. But if, as the angels have proclaimed, growth comes out of embracing differences, could we achieve lasting peace through embracing the differences between us instead of fighting over them? We have surely not been able to bring it about through consensus. We don't have consensus in this realm, not really. We don't even agree about the Spirit.

"We each approach the Spirit in a different way, with different understandings. We claim to be a unified Church and to have a unity of belief, but we don't really have that now and we never really had it in the past. Perhaps to be human is to be in disagreement. Perhaps to experience peace as a human is to glory in the beauty of disagreement. Agreement has brought peace to the Realm of Light but there is still an emptiness in their relationships. They long for relationships with those who are different from themselves. They come to our realm seeking that and now, at last, we are ready to respond. The veil between the realms is being lifted. Does peace stand at the conjunction of the two realms? Is peace found where the Realm of Light meets the Physical Realm? Is peace found at the conjunction of two different ways of being?

"I'm not quite sure what I'm seeking but I think there is something here that we are supposed to find together. I think the Spirit brought us together for a reason other than merely to satisfy our desire for intimacy or power or meaning or peace. Oriental religions speak of the power of the Yin and the Yang, the coming together of opposites. We have never had that coming together of opposites in a complete sense until now. Perhaps we now have the Yin and the Yang in the merging of our two realms. Could it be that *The Kingdom* is the coming together of two opposite realms, producing harmony in the universe, not out of agreement but out of difference. Our realm has always been incomplete. The Realm of Light has, I suspect, also been incomplete. The prophecies are of a new creation; a new heaven and a new earth. As we, in our realm, get glimpses of what it is like to operate without time and the Beings of

Light experience glimpses of reality with time, and as we humans learn to operate with the unrestricted creative powers of the mind, and the Beings of Light learn to operate with physical restrictions, are we not both encountering a new way of being, a new heaven and a new earth?"

James sat down.

A Being, whom Jonathan had not previously met, spoke to the group mentally. "There is an expectation in the Realm of Light that when the merger comes it will bring with it a great period of confusion culminating in a season of rapid growth and fulfillment for all beings engaged in the endeavor. The nature of that confusion and the exact nature of the subsequent growth have never been fully explained to us. There has been some speculation about it among our teachers but none of them seem to really know any specifics. Yin and Yang are not principles that we are familiar with directly, because we do not experience opposites in our realm. We do have a concept of difference, however, that is spoken of in *The Holy Body of Knowledge*. It says there that 'difference is to be encountered, to be valued, and to be loved.'

"Since we, too, are moving toward a merger with the Spirit, the value of difference has never made much sense to us. We had assumed that our difference from the Spirit was something to be abhorred and that the difference from each other was contrary to *The Way of Peace*. It occurs to me, however, that *The Holy Body of Knowledge* may be prophetic. It may be speaking of a period, such as this one, when the opportunity to interact in-depth with beings from a different realm is made available to us. The glory of difference may not be in finding differences among ourselves but in exploring the differences between us and those in your realm. Perhaps it is those differences that are life-giving; those differences that deepen our awareness of the Spirit. Then we may find the true meaning of the verse that says, 'it is between the differences that similarity with the Spirit is encountered.' Is it possible that beings from our realm and yours can all find the Spirit, not in our similarities with the Spirit, but in the differences that exist between us?"

"What does that mean?" asked another Being of Light.

"Excuse me," said the abbot. "If you don't mind me interrupting for a moment, it occurs to me that some of us from this realm may not yet be able to hear the communications of the Beings of Light. Is that the case?"

Two monks indicated that they had heard nothing but silence after James' statement. The abbot explained what had transpired, and then spoke to the Beings again. "That brings up a question I have that may be related to this whole issue of difference. Why is it that some of us can see and hear you while others cannot?"

"The difference is in us, not in you," said the Being who had just spoken.

"I'm afraid I don't understand," said the abbot.

"The difference has no meaning on your level. Those who hear or see are in no way superior to those who do not. We select certain ones of you to relate to because of our own needs for growth in certain areas and it is to those ones that we impart the ability to see or to hear us. That has caused much confusion in your realm because in the past there was a tendency for those in your realm to venerate those individuals who had seen us or spoken to us. The ability to see or to hear us is not a sign of spiritual superiority; it is merely an indication that we have chosen to work with you. The difference of abilities that some of you appear to have is not really a difference at all. The difference in your abilities is an illusion."

"I'm getting hopelessly confused," said one of the Beings.

"I am too," said another.

"I think we are all a little confused," said a third.

"I'm confused about what you are confused about," said

a fourth.

"And I'm confused about why you seem not to be confused," retorted another.

"It appears to me that the period of confusion has started," said the Being who had originally spoken immediately after James. "Perhaps we need to disengage for a period and regroup."

"An excellent idea," agreed yet another being.

The Beings faded from view.

"Perhaps we have all had enough confusion for one night," said the abbot. "I understand that James, Francis and Jonathan have each had considerable experience with the Beings in the past. Is there anything more that you would like to add to this before we end our meeting tonight?"

James shook his head.

Francis rose. "I think we have just begun to scratch the surface of this subject. I'm quite anxious to hear more from James about what he has learned, and I am very willing to share with you what I have learned. It would also be helpful to have more meetings with some Beings of Light in attendance, as we did tonight. But I, for one, am exhausted." He turned to James. "James, I've lost a lot of sleep over you lately and I'm too old to stay up all night and then be bright and chipper the next day. The next time you decide to take a fall, you are on your own." They all laughed.

"Let's bring things to a close tonight," said the abbot. "I think we all need some rest. We will continue this discussion at a later time."

Someone suggested that they all meet again the following evening. There was quick and enthusiastic agreement. The abbot led them in an abbreviated form of Compline, the traditional evening service, and bid them all a good night.

CHAPTER 25

The next day, the morning Eucharist was again filled with power and the presence of angels. In the afternoon, when Francis and Jonathan were meeting together, Azar appeared.

"Am I intruding?" he asked.

"Absolutely not! Welcome!" said Francis. "I would offer you a chair but, as you can see, there aren't any extras. Would you like to sit here on the edge of the bed?"

Jonathan stood. "You can have my chair if you like, Azar."

"No, Jonathan, please sit down. One of the advantages of not having a physical body is that I can sit anywhere." He seated himself comfortably in the open space in front of the door, his body suspended in space as though held up by an imaginary lounge chair.

"We were just talking about the issue of peace and the coming of *The Kingdom*," said Jonathan.

"I know," replied Azar. "That's why I came. If you are going to be helpful to others, there are some more things that you need to understand."

"Azar," said Jonathan, "before we get into that, may I ask you a question?"

"Certainly, Jonathan."

"I have been wondering." Jonathan continued. "Azar, I am usually a very impatient person. But I am amazingly patient when I am with you. I put up with your long-winded ramblings with very little difficulty now. But more than that, I have noticed that I feel more settled, more whole, more at peace when I am with you."

"So, what's your question, Jonathan?"

"My question is, why am I more at peace when I am with you?"

"Why?"

"Yes, why? I'm different when I'm with you."

"It's your resonance, Jonathan."

"My resonance?"

"Yes. Have you noticed that your energy shifts to a different vibration rate when you come into the presence of Beings of Light?"

"Well yes, come to think of it, it does. That occurred when you visited me in my realm also. It was subtle but I did notice it."

"That's part of what I was going to explain to you. All beings in your realm function better when they are in our presence, but it is more noticeable in some people than it is in others. The point is that you can not truly achieve inner peace or peace in the world without our presence.

"Peace occurs at a different frequency than war. Jonathan, you must understand that how I am explaining this is not exactly the way it is, but it is as close as I can come using the terminology and concepts that are familiar to you in your realm. As I was saying, true peace has a different vibration rate, a different resonance, than war. The resonance of peace is not natural to your realm. If we are not present, despite your best intentions, you will slip into activities that are more in harmony with your normal vibration rate. That is why those in your realm keep returning to war even when they are trying intellectually to achieve peace.

"The Spirit created your realm with the plan that your realm and our realm would eventually be merged. You need us and we need you. In order to experience the deepest levels of your being, within your own realm, you must enter into our presence. People need to invite us to be a part of their lives. They need to ask for our aid. We are always ready to help but asking us to help greatly increases the level of our involvement. One of the tasks that all humans share in common is their need to fully discover their involvement with all other beings, both visible and invisible. It is that that brings *wholeness*, not learning to be an 'individual.' We have talked in depth about the need for your realm and our realm to be joined, but there is also a need for each person in your realm to join with those of us who are assigned to care for your well-being.

"People are not truly whole until they discover that no one is really an individual. Separateness is an illusion. Communion is the reality. Love is the recognition and expression of that union. You love another person when you recognize that they are a part of you. You come to love us when you fulfill your destiny of allowing us to be a part of you and you of us.

"Jonathan, you are incomplete without us. You are unable, on your own, without our presence, to maintain the vibration, the frequency, of true inner or outer peace. All emotions, all feelings, have a frequency. We assist you in raising your vibrations so that you can achieve peace and love in your hearts. You must be in communion with us in order to be fully in communion with yourself. You fear giving up control of your life. You fear being vulnerable. But it is vulnerability that makes you truly open and it is in the context of vulnerability that we, the Beings of Light, come and remain.

"I also want to explain something about rituals because there are many people in your realm who misunderstand the purpose of religious rites. Some rituals celebrate an existing reality, others are anticipatory celebrations of that which is to come. The Eucharistic celebration you attended in this monastery has primarily been an anticipatory celebration of the coming union of the visible with the invisible, the future joining of your realm with our realm. Today, it also became a celebration of the merger that has started to unfold, a celebration of the coming of *The Kingdom on Earth* as it is in Heaven.

"Peace is *The Kingdom*, Jonathan. It is not just that *The Kingdom* will bring peace. *The Kingdom* is peace. And it is a peace that is far more profound than the absence of conflict. The peace that comes with the merger is a peace 'that passes all understanding' and involves the coming together of all that *IS* in a new form. Peace between nations can now evolve because the union of the two realms is underway. The union releases a kind of energy, a different sort of vibration, that those in your realm can choose to align with or not."

"Can you say more about that Azar? I'm not sure I fully understand," said Jonathan.

"Yes. In the past, peace in your realm has been associated with inactivity, with lack of conflict, not with strength. War was experienced as a powerful force, but peace was not. The absence of war tended to be thought of as peace. But the absence of war is not peace. Peace is a force that is more powerful than war. It's energy, although more subtle, is stronger than the coarser energy of war.

"Jonathan, there is really no way I can explain all this in the language in which you presently communicate. The energy I am talking about is not really fine or coarse and it doesn't quite have to do with vibrations either. You don't yet have any accurate terms in your language I can use to explain that. The age of peace will bring with it a new understanding of human dynamics and energy flow. Peace will come to be understood in a new way and its power will be recognized as it has never been recognized before.

"Peace is a force and love is a force, but they are not the same. It is important to understand that. You must also understand that there are ways of pursuing peace, of following its energy flow, that are not related to the rules of non-engagement at all.

"Let me explain. You have tended to look on peace as the absence of war or the absence of conflict. But conflict or the absence of it has nothing whatsoever to do with peace. Peace comes out of living in alignment with the power of peace, not out of the resolution of conflict. Conflict can exist quite comfortably in a state of peace. Nations can have quite different understandings of very important issues and yet be in a state of absolute and total peace with each other. In the past, many leaders in your realm have put energy into efforts to resolve conflict because they assumed that the resolution of conflict was the path to peace.

"Do you remember James' mention of the Yin and Yang principle? As one of us said last night, we do not have those concepts, but we do have peace. Peace does not emerge out of the resolution of conflict. Conflict does not exist for us. Confusion, yes, but conflict, no. The Yin and the Yang principle does have value in helping to explain what I am trying to tell you because it deals with the harmony of opposites. That is not the same as the resolution of conflict. Conflict is not what Yin and Yang are about. That principle is about two types of forces in the universe that must exist in balance. It is the balance of the two forces that helps to bring about peace.

"What I am trying to tell you, Jonathan, is that conflict can exist quite comfortably within a state of peace. Conflict is not the enemy of peace; it is the power behind peace. I realize that it may be hard for you to understand or accept what I am telling you now, but it is quite true. One of the reasons peace has been unattainable in your realm is that conflict has not been harnessed as the energy behind peace. You have been resisting the very thing that has the power to give you that which you are seeking.

"The merger is necessary. It is not until the merger

occurs that the conflict between our two quite different realms will be strong enough to generate the necessary energy to bring about peace.

"I don't know how to explain this to you, Jonathan, but it is essential that you understand it because the future of your world depends on it. Is what I have been telling you any clearer than it was?"

"Yes, a little, but I still find it confusing," said Jonathan. "I don't fully understand it."

"I'm not surprised. This is not easy to grasp, especially since your language has not evolved enough in this area to make communication easy.

"Jonathan, the resolution of conflict is not important. In fact, the resolution of conflict makes peace more difficult to achieve because the energy is not there to empower the peace process. The Spirit allows conflict and even enjoys it. If that were not the case the Spirit would never have approved of the merger of your realm with ours. The power of the conflict, Jonathan.... It is the power of the conflict of two opposing realms that allows peace to break forth in your world. Peace comes out of that conflict. There is no way you can resolve the conflict between your realm and ours. There is no way you can become an angel but, because of the merger, you will be able to more freely experience the differences. For brief periods you can experience existence as we do but there is no way that you can operate for long outside of the sphere of time nor can you sit as I am doing in empty space for long without expending vast amounts of energy.

"Jonathan, peace is the Spirit's gift to those who are in conflict. It is not a gift given to those who are trying to avoid suffering. It is your longing to be like an angel and to experience existence as we experience it that will give you the power to experience peace. We have peace because we long to be human but cannot be fully human. The merger does not decrease the conflict, Jonathan; it intensifies it! That is what this is all about. That is the secret behind *The Kingdom*. It has come here. It looks like harmony. We come together in the services now and we can meet together, as we did last night, whenever we choose. But it is out of the conflict that we are empowered. It is out of our differences that we experience fulfillment.

"Yin and Yang. They are not the resolution of conflict. They are not the doing away with difference. Harmony is not achieved through agreement and meaning does not come through comfort. The Yin and the Yang are the power of the opposites. Do not ever try to do away with opposites; glory in their power. The power is found between them. And the power of peace is generated out of the differences between our realms. Our longing to be human puts us at peace. Your longing to be like us can help you achieve peace. You never will be like us, Jonathan. Even in the afterlife you will not be fully like us. But you will find peace in the difference.

"That is what you need to tell others in your realm, Jonathan. Suffering will not be ended by the coming of peace, but the suffering will be glorious. Nations can exist without war now, but they cannot exist in that state for long unless the people long to be like us and draw close to us and seek to learn from us. We are here to give and to serve. We are here to show you the path to peace, but you will have to find it in the midst of conflict and inner yearnings. The Spirit created you to be human in this life but also to long to be like us. When you allow that longing to fully emerge, you and all the people will be at peace and the nations of the world, though different, will be able to live together in harmony."

Francis broke in, "I don't fully understand all this, Azar."

"You do not have to understand it, Francis. Your work is here. If you come to understand it, that's fine. But it is not necessary.

"Jonathan's work is in the world beyond this monastery

and he is the one who must help others to understand.

"Do you understand it now, Jonathan?"

"Yes, I believe so."

"Do you long to be like us?"

"Yes, Azar, I long for that with all my heart."

"Then you are on the path to peace, Jonathan, and my work is finished."

"Will I see you no more? I have grown very fond of you, Azar."

"And I of you, Jonathan. You are my dearest friend. Oh, you'll see me around all right. I don't forget my friends. Together we have helped to change the course of human history. But I'm finished with this two-bit job as a tour guide.

"Jonathan, I have been thinking; with all this new interest in angels that is emerging in your realm, we could do quite well for ourselves if we went into business together selling angel wings. What do you think, Jonathan? Do we really have to tell them that angels don't have wings?"

Author's Biography

Patton Boyle and his wife live in Wenatchee, Washington, where he continues to write books about spiritual growth and discovery. His first book, *Screaming Hawk: The Mystic Warrior,* has been published in English, French, German, and Greek.

His other novels, Screaming Hawk: The Mystic Paths, Screaming Hawk: The Mystic Teacher, Screaming Hawk: The Mystic Healer, and a short book for Children, The Land of Joy, are also available on Amazon in e-book and paperback format.

The author can be contacted at
pattonboyle1@gmail.com.

www.ingramcontent.com/pod-product-compliance
Lightning Source LLC
Chambersburg PA
CBHW031547040426
42452CB00006B/228